Cambridge Elements

COSTLY OPPORTUNITIES

Social Mobility in Segregated Societies

María José Álvarez-Rivadulla
Universidad de los Andes

Shaftesbury Road, Cambridge CB2 8EA, United Kingdom

One Liberty Plaza, 20th Floor, New York, NY 10006, USA

477 Williamstown Road, Port Melbourne, VIC 3207, Australia

314–321, 3rd Floor, Plot 3, Splendor Forum, Jasola District Centre, New Delhi – 110025, India

103 Penang Road, #05–06/07, Visioncrest Commercial, Singapore 238467

Cambridge University Press is part of Cambridge University Press & Assessment, a department of the University of Cambridge.

We share the University's mission to contribute to society through the pursuit of education, learning and research at the highest international levels of excellence.

www.cambridge.org
Information on this title: www.cambridge.org/9781009503204

DOI: 10.1017/9781009503242

When citing this work, please include a reference to the DOI 10.1017/9781009503242

First published 2024

A catalogue record for this publication is available from the British Library.

ISBN 978-1-009-50320-4 Hardback
ISBN 978-1-009-50323-5 Paperback
ISSN 2515-5253 (online)
ISSN 2515-5245 (print)

Costly Opportunities

Social Mobility in Segregated Societies

Elements in Politics and Society in Latin America

DOI: 10.1017/9781009503242
First published online: April 2024

María José Álvarez-Rivadulla
Universidad de los Andes

Author for correspondence: María José Álvarez-Rivadulla, mj.alvarez@uniandes.edu.co

Abstract: This Element investigates entrenched inequality in Latin America through a unique case of class integration in Colombian higher education. Examining a forgivable loan program benefiting 40,000 high-achieving individuals from disadvantaged backgrounds, the Element introduces "gate opening" and "diversified networks" as mechanisms countering traditional inequality reproduction. Utilizing a longitudinal, ethnographic approach, it explores the evolving process of social mobility within an elite school, emphasizing subjective experiences and challenges. Despite educational gaps and stark social differences, most students formed cross-class friendships, completed their education, and achieved higher socioeconomic positions. Yet, in so doing, they had to face several mobility associated costs, and they faced them resourcing to strategies such as camouflaging or disclosing, sometimes becoming culturally omnivorous in the end. The significance of a prestigious degree varies based on the professional labor market, with first-generation students facing more challenges in low-quality or elitist markets where cultural and social capital act as entry barriers.

This Element also has a video abstract: www.cambridge.org/PSLT_Alvarez

Keywords: social capital, social mobility, social class, inequality, segregation

ISBNs: 9781009503204 (HB), 9781009503235 (PB), 9781009503242 (OC)
ISSNs: 2515-5253 (online), 2515-5245 (print)

Contents

Preface

I have been interested in, and preoccupied by, inequality ever since I remember. Yet, and perhaps oddly, I had never thought of my own history of mobility or questioned my own social class. It was only when this Uruguayan, daughter of uneducated Spanish peasant migrants, arrived in Colombia that she felt the weight and privilege of social class. Just by having university education, and a PhD by then, I had access to more goods in Colombia than I would in Uruguay. A better salary. A better neighborhood. More prestige. Back in Uruguay, I had never felt any different from my school friends, some of them sons or daughters of professionals. We all went to the same state elementary school, and, although there were no books at my home, there were plenty at my friend's house in the same block. In Colombia none of my friends went to state school. That makes a difference.

I never felt disadvantaged at university, being a first-generation student. I never even thought of myself in those terms. It was only when I met and started studying the main characters of this Element, *the Ser Pilo Paga* recipients, that I started comparing and understanding my own experience. Yes, my mother felt ashamed for not knowing how to sign public documents, but that was never a barrier for me. I consistently maintained good grades, and I never once doubted my ability to attend university. I never experienced discrimination, and I always felt at home, both in college and in any other environment.

I am not idealizing my home country here. Following a tradition of sociological inquiry initiated by Carlos Filgueira and Ruben Kaztman, I have been one of the voices denouncing and studying inequality and segregation in Uruguayan society, particularly in urban and educational spaces. The educational disparities in Uruguay are indeed striking. Yet, despite this, both inequality and segregation are even more pronounced in Colombian society. Barriers to mobility are higher as well, even for exceptional people in exceptional contexts such as high achievers with an all-inclusive scholarship. And yet, it was in this unequal context that a scholarship for high-achieving, low-income students emerged, offering an unprecedented opportunity to observe their trajectories into higher education and, subsequently, into the labor market.

This Element tells their story and reflects upon both the power of opportunity and the enduring obstacles that make people feel they do not belong or push them further down the social ladder. The narrative is full of grays, as social reality often is. It unveils the cracks in the meritocratic discourse, and the formal and informal barriers that inhibit even the most talented people coming from disadvantaged groups from moving up the social ladder. Yet, at the same time, it shows a realm of possibility. It demonstrates that de-segregation is possible even late in life and within highly fragmented societies. It reveals that connections can form across class boundaries among young people who, despite leading disparate lives, come together in educational settings. It underscores how education can profoundly transform lives, producing positive ripple effects for families and communities. The Element also emphasizes the influential role of public policy and the transformative power of opportunity.

To Paola, Kevin, Elkin, Wendy, Angie, Juan Camilo, Cristian, Leonardo, Sergio, and all of you who made it against all odds. Thank you for making me feel I had something to teach you. You have no idea of how much you have enriched my thinking as a researcher and my sense of purpose in life as a person. For more first-generation students. And lower mobility costs.

1 Introduction

> When Ana Sofía was invited to a party in an affluent neighborhood in the North of Bogotá during her first semester in college, she learned firsthand what privilege really meant. She had been recalibrating inequality since she entered this elite college, although of course she knew that she belonged to the lower part of the distribution in a very unequal society. After overcoming her initial fears of discrimination, she felt welcomed and stimulated in an environment that valued "being a nerd," as she puts it. Yet, she no longer felt at the top of her class as she had done at high school. In fact, she had been feeling somewhat behind, especially because she lacked proficiency in English, unlike some of her bilingual classmates, which most professors took for granted. Yet, her excursion to the North marked a significant shift in her understanding of inequality.
>
> First of all, she said, the living room the party was held in was the size of her entire house. Second, everybody was extremely kind to her. She felt very welcomed but found the sociability of the upper class, which involved "giving kisses to everybody and using pet names" to be foreign to her. "Nobody calls me Sofi elsewhere," she remarked, in contrast to the rougher sociability she was used to in her high school. And, finally, she discovered, as she eloquently put it, "the rich too listen to *reggeaton*!"
>
> This encounter, and even more so the relationship between Ana Sofía and her new privileged classmates, would have never happened in an unequal and fragmented society such as the Colombian one, if not for the government scholarship that Ana Sofia had won. The *Ser Pilo Paga* [Being Smart Pays and SPP hereafter] program was designed to enable high-achieving, low-income students to access high-quality colleges, and it significantly contributed to enhancing class diversity in elite colleges, particularly the one she attended. Ana Sofía felt more comfortable around other scholarship recipients who, as she described, "speak like me, joke around, and laugh." However, during her five years in college, she also formed a few friendships with middle-class students. While she defined these ties as "more rational, more academic, less intimate," she valued them because she learned from them and wanted them to be part of her university experience. Yet, making cross-class acquaintances and friends in elite college environments requires work, and this hidden relational burden lays overwhelmingly on the shoulders of

> underprivileged students. As this case evinces, it is Ana Sofia who has to travel across the city (unlike in the United States, in Colombia it is not common for students to live in dorms,), learn the social norms, adjust, and bear the financial expenses of buying the appropriate clothes for a party, paying for lunch at upscale food outlets, or, even more difficult, acknowledging that she does not have the means to join in certain activities.
>
> Ana Sofía is the first college graduate in her family and is currently the main provider in her household which includes her two siblings, mother, and grandmother. She works as a researcher for a big academic project, a position she secured through a recommendation from one of her professors. She also engages in consultancy work, often overworking, to meet her ultimate goal of saving to buy a home for her family. Attending Study University and making contacts there played a pivotal role in her upward mobility. Yet, as we will see, this upward trajectory came with its own set of challenges and sacrifices.

We know Latin America is a lopsided continent in which institutions are fragmented or exclusionary, our cities and schools segregated, and social mobility unlikely (Benza & Kessler, 2020). We know much less about the everyday mechanisms that sustain these structures of entrenched inequality and immobility, and, even less so, about the changes we can make to erode them. This Element delves into these mechanisms by examining an unconventional case of class integration and social mobility in higher education in Colombia. It follows the recipients of a forgivable loan program that disrupted the social composition of elite universities by providing 40,000 high-achieving youngsters from disadvantaged backgrounds with access to higher education, from their initial enrollment in college to their first jobs.

While economics, development studies, and, from a practical perspective, international agencies and governments view education as the solution for the region's growth and the social mobility of its people, sociology suggests that education tends to perpetuate rather than alter inequalities. Schools and families often transmit social class to students and children through the inculcation of ingrained dispositions that determine how people perceive their social environment and respond to it (habitus) (Bourdieu, 1998; Lareau, 2011). Children from less privileged families typically attend schools with fewer resources, while middle- and upper-class children, benefiting from greater educational and economic resources at home, attend superior schools, exacerbating the divide. Even when some disadvantaged individuals manage to gain admission to elite institutions, exclusionary practices make mobility either exceedingly rare or unattainable.

This is true on many occasions, but the prevalent lens of reproduction can obscure instances of social change when they occur. Without idealizing the policy experiment at the heart of this research, this Element uses it to shed light on two mechanisms that mitigate inequality and promote social mobility: gate opening and diversified networks. Like Streib (2017), I believe that our theoretical toolkit is unbalanced when it comes to understanding mobility versus reproduction. Yet, unlike her interesting emphasis on the cultural traits that may foster mobility, which I value and incorporate, my main theoretical contribution in this Element is more relational. The two mechanisms I explore here are the other side of the coin of Tilly's (1998) theory of the mechanisms responsible of producing and reproducing categorical inequality, that is, exploitation, opportunity hoarding, emulation, and adaptation. *Gate opening* is the direct opposite to opportunity hoarding. While the former refers to easing access to valued resources through letting the previously excluded in, the latter guarantees closure around privilege. *Diversified networks*, in turn, disrupt adaptation to regular, unequal, homophilic relations. Adaptation, according to Tilly, involves devising procedures that perpetuate daily interactions, sustaining inequality, and forming valued social relations around existing divisions. When, for various reasons, individuals with unequal resources come together and they form unlikely diverse networks, inequality may change. Having friends with more resources increases the likelihood of social mobility (Chetty et al., 2022; Coleman, 1988).

Besides showing these mechanisms in action and doing so from the perspective of those benefiting from them over an extended period of time, I also highlight the structural barriers to profiting from them and from being able to break the entrenched patterns of inequality and reproduction in deeply fragmented contexts. On the one hand, I illustrate how, following an instance of gate opening that allows previously excluded individuals to enter, subsequent instances of opportunity hoarding may exclude them again (with university dropouts being the clearest example in this case, and, later, poor-quality and elitist labor markets can reintroduce significant inequalities). On the other hand, I demonstrate the costs of building diversified networks, which are by no means a natural consequence of merely mixing different groups in the same environments, even if this mixing is a necessary condition for nonsegregated networks to develop. These costs tend to be borne by the poorest individuals rather than by the institutions or those who benefit from the ease of privilege. I refer to these costs as "relational costs," and they pertain to the expenses of constructing diversified social capital. These costs accumulate and differ from those more commonly emphasized in the literature, such as the cultural capital costs of adapting to the norms, assumptions, and behaviors prevalent in elite institutions and environments.

The longitudinal approach of this Element provides a closer look at the process of social mobility as it unfolds, allowing us to observe its evolution over time and identify the factors that either facilitate or hinder it. Its ethnographic perspective enables a seamless transition from the macro indicators to the micro-processes, shedding light on the subjective perspectives, anxieties, aspirations, and emotions of those undergoing class mobility in comparison to their families of origin. It also allows for comparisons with those who have enjoyed the privilege of a more stable position in the middle or upper classes. This Element is the result of an eight-year multimethod project conducted at an elite university that included 104 interviews with students from different social classes, with several of them interviewed at least twice over time. Additionally, a two-wave network survey was administered to students majoring in four different disciplines, and informal conversations and presentations were held with different members of the college community. This Element also draws on existing secondary information about higher education and social mobility in Colombia and in the region.

The findings of this Element both support and challenge some of the prevailing beliefs about the role of education in social mobility. They reveal the complexities inherent in the process. On the one hand, it underscores the remarkable power of opening previously closed opportunity gates, providing real-life narratives that illustrate the transformative potential of higher education for many students who may never have had the chance to attend a top-tier institution without programs like the one examined in this study. Yet, at the same time, it highlights the persistent influence of years of accumulated disadvantages and the formidable challenges they present, especially in highly class-segregated societies. These societies are "strongly penetrated by hierarchical socio-cultural matrices, matrices that resist any progress of inclusive development models" (Kaztman, 2023), resulting in substantial costs even for those who do manage to achieve successful social mobility.

1.1 Daniel

From the perspective of the university and the government statistics, Daniel is considered a success story. Born and raised in the poorest locality of Bogotá, he finished his law degree in one of the country's best private universities. His parents own a stationary store and internet café where he helped out throughout his university years and after graduation for a while. They have always invested in his education, including sending him to a nearby private school and having high expectations for his academic success. As discussed in Section 2, families and professors are crucial in shaping the habitus and trajectories of high-achieving students from disadvantaged backgrounds like Daniel. While his family instilled aspirations for upward mobility through education, which does not align with a framework of habitus reproduction, they simply could not afford to send him to Study University had it not been for the SPP Scholarship he won due to his exceptional performance in the end-of-school state exam. Despite now proudly proclaiming on his social media profiles that he graduated as a "*becado* from Ciudad Bolívar," the processes of adapting to and completing college were far from straightforward. He used to hide his neighborhood. Initially, he

> concealed his neighborhood background and would say, "I'm from the South," without specifying Ciudad Bolívar out of fear of facing discrimination. In the beginning, he tried to camouflage and hide his origins. His trajectory mirrors that of many students we encountered who initially harbored feelings of shame or fear but gradually transformed them into pride. When looking at the present "outcome," a proud, college-educated young lawyer from an underprivileged background, the often challenging path he traversed becomes invisible.
>
> He was a student in one of my classes and when he heard about my research on the program he was a fellow of, Daniel stayed after class and, with tears in his eyes, told me his story. Another day, and in the privacy of my office, he cried again and repeatedly verbalized his emotions during the two hours we were together. He described his first day as an ordeal. "I thought about what clothes I should wear," he sobbed. "What if they laughed at my clothes?" He was very self-conscious. In contrast to some of his future classmates that came from elite high schools and already knew each other, he was the only one from his high school to win the scholarship to be able to attend one of the most expensive tuition fees in the country. It was difficult to make friends. At the time, Daniel was determined to keep his scholarship status a secret. He was afraid that regular students would view someone from a disadvantaged background with suspicion. "When they look at me, I want them to think, 'he pays,'" he told me. Since he entered college, he bought new clothes, to the extent of incurring debt for it at one point. He even began straightening his hair every day. His efforts to belong, assimilate, and conceal his true background demanded daily effort, but he believes this effort has ultimately paid off.

Daniel was not the only one crying in an interview. Many people did, including those listening to our preliminary findings or reading early drafts of the work. "Your article brought tears to my eyes. That's my story too," said a professor from a working-class background that had studied at the same elite university a long time ago. A graduate student I have not personally met recently sent me an email expressing their gratitude. "Thank you. I have identified with some of your informants. I have felt their emotions. Your articles are therapeutic." I am not a sociologist specializing in emotions and had not anticipated this aspect in my fieldwork. I had conducted interviewed with individuals from much poorer backgrounds in the outskirts of Montevideo, Bogotá, and Medellín but these emotions did not surface. It turned out that the interviews, articles, and press appearances have stirred the "hidden injuries of class" (Sennett & Cobb, 1972). They have elicited the "emotional costs of becoming different" (Reay, 2005). Social mobility, especially when it is rapid and long-range (Bourdieu, 1998, 2007; Friedman, 2014, 2016) and, I would add, when it happens in segregated contexts, incurs emotional and other costs. Section 3 addresses these costs, paying particular attention to the relational costs of making friends and cross-class ties.

> Graduating made Daniel feel proud and able, even though it took him more semesters than it should have, and he had to ask for a loan to be able to finish because the scholarship did not cover those extra semesters. As I describe in Section 4, finding work was not easy either, and led to much frustration and disappointment. He faced obstacles in certain elitist areas of law, such as law firms, where his lack of cultural and social capital became apparent. And, public jobs in law were difficult to come by. Unlike his more affluent fellow graduates who could easily get jobs even before graduation or survive on their parents while looking for a good opportunity, he had to pay his debt and help his parents. Not being able to find a job, he decided to apply for another loan and do an MA abroad instead, in the meantime. I wrote a recommendation letter for him. He passed. Despite his financial obligations, he finished his MA already and will stay on to do his PhD.

Daniel's story illustrates the complexities of social mobility. If we only take the start and end points, as is often done in social mobility studies, Daniel is clearly a success. He has achieved higher levels of education than his parents and from a prestigious institution. However, (chutes) a closer examination of the longitudinal ethnographic data uncovers the snakes and ladders that can either propel or hinder social mobility. It also sheds light on the subjective processes and experiences of individuals navigating social mobility as the journey unfolds.

1.2 Mobility, (Higher) Education, and Segregation

Upward social mobility involves the movement of individuals from more disadvantaged backgrounds to higher positions on the social ladder. It is often associated with positive changes, from life opportunities to subjective well-being (Chan, 2018). Higher education often plays a crucial role in facilitating social mobility, but this often depends on the extent to which the context provides access, retention, and employment opportunities for graduates of diverse backgrounds (Beller & Hout, 2006; Billingham, 2018). Latin American societies tend to have lower levels of educational (Hertz et al., 2007) and income mobility (Torche, 2014) than more affluent societies, despite the almost doubling of the number of students in higher education programs in the region since 2000, and efforts to make access more equitable (Ferreyra, Avitabile, & Paz, 2017).

Higher education is becoming more diverse worldwide. Even elite colleges are opening their doors to more students from different backgrounds, through affirmative action policies, scholarships, loans, and other types of national, local, or institutional policies. In the United States for example, Ivy League Universities, which have faced criticism for their historical exclusionary practices, are actively promoting their diversity (Lee, 2016). In Latin America, some countries have implemented specific policies to increase access to elite education for underprivileged groups. These policies include affirmative action for Afro-Brazilian students in Brazil (Valente & Berry, 2017), subsidies in Peru (Adrianzén, Chevez, Morales, Quevedo, & Chiyón, 2019; Cotler, 2016) similar policies in Colombia and the introduction of free higher education in Chile (Espinoza & González, 2016). Understanding the experiences of lower-class students after they enter universities is crucial to improving their experience, ensuring retention, and promoting social mobility. Does high-quality higher education succeed in leveling the basic inequalities that exist between students from different socioeconomic backgrounds? What happens after access? These questions are the focus of Section 3, dedicated particularly to analyzing and developing the concept of relational costs, which refers to the costs of building friendships, especially with more privileged peers, which can increase the social capital of underprivileged.

Besides educational opportunities, diversified networks can play a critical role in social mobility. Recent research by Chetty and his co-authors (2022) has shed light on a topic with a long tradition in sociology (Coleman, 1988) and that inspired this research: the role of social capital in social mobility. With novel evidence and methodological creativity their work reveals that growing up in environments with more interclass connections is beneficial for those with fewer resources as it increases their likelihood of achieving social mobility.

In class-segregated societies such as the ones often found in Latin America, opportunities for achieving social mobility via this mechanism of interclass connections have always been limited and are becoming even scarcer. Neighborhoods, schools, and public spaces are becoming increasingly more class segregated, even in societies with traditionally more cross-class interactions like the Southern Cone ones (Kaztman, 2001). As Saraví (2015) describes for the case of Mexico, youth from different socioeconomic backgrounds often have distinct and separate life trajectories and very rarely cross paths. The city they inhabit, their consumption spaces, and their schools are worlds apart. This is what makes the experiment this Element is based on, the *SPP* program, so unique.

Yet, the path to social mobility extends beyond higher education and into the labor market, where new barriers and opportunities may emerge, and existing evidence presents a mixed picture. While some studies highlight the leveling role of higher education in the labor market (Chetty et al. 2020; Manzoni & Streib, 2019; Torche, 2011), others highlight the specific barriers present in certain labor markets, in particular the additional role of cultural or social capital, regardless of education, to enter elite occupations which require a certain "pedigree" (Rivera, 2016) and have a "class ceiling" (Friedman & Laurison, 2019).

This study is one of the few (Bathmaker et al., 2016; Ingram et al., 2023; Royster, 2003) – and the only one in the region to my knowledge – following students from when they enter college through their transition to the labor market. This extended perspective allows me to observe the process and the mechanisms that either perpetuate inequality or facilitate mobility as they occur over a substantial period of time. This timeline encompasses two turning points: entering school and entering the labor market. As mentioned earlier, this study unveils the effectiveness of two mechanisms: gate opening (which eases access to university and later to a promising job market for degree holders) and diversified networks (which foster integration and later establish contacts for the labor market). While focusing on these virtuous mechanisms, the study also emphasizes the costs of social mobility in each part of the process.

1.3 Colombia and Its Opportunity Opening and Mixing Experiment

With a Gini index of 0.51 (World Bank, 2021), Colombia is the eleventh most unequal country in the world. Although recent years have witnessed a considerable decrease in poverty and a much more modest reduction in inequality, the COVID-19 pandemic dramatically increased monetary poverty (to 42.5 percent of the population according to the National Statistics Department DANE in 2021), exacerbating inequality once more. Colombia continues to exhibit a particularly high association between parents' and their children's education, especially when compared to similar countries in the region (Angulo, Gaviria, Páez, & Azevedo, 2012; Behrman, Gaviria, Székely, Birdsall, & Galiani, 2001; García, Rodríguez, Sánchez, & Bedoya, 2015). Besides high levels of inequality and limited social mobility, Colombia is also a deeply socially segregated society, particularly at the upper echelons of society. In terms of education, class segregation has been a long-standing issue. Public education was originally established to cater to the needs of the poor (García-Villegas, Cárdenas, & Fergusson, 2021). The rich and the poor have rarely shared educational spaces, leading some authors to speak of an educational apartheid, considering elementary and secondary schooling (García-Villegas & López, 2011).

Although the rate of students attending higher education has been growing in Colombia, reaching a surprising 53.9 percent (SNIES, 2021), access is still profoundly class segregated, especially if we consider access to what the Ministry of Education classifies as high-quality institutions. There is a strong correlation between socioeconomic status and results in the end-of-high-school state exam (Saber 11), which determines students' access to many high-quality universities. Despite the majority of students taking the state exam (Saber 11) belonging to the lower strata, the ones achieving high scores and entering universities primarily come from more affluent backgrounds. Only 5 percent of students from the lowest official socioeconomic category (*Estrato* 1) score in the top decile of the exam distribution (Álvarez-Rivadulla et al., 2017, data from 2012 to 2015). Moreover, due to other barriers (additional and challenging entrance exams, financial constraints, relocation needs, work commitments, limited scholarship opportunities, apprehension toward loans, etc.), even those outliers from the lower SES who do well on the state exam do not enjoy guaranteed access to high-quality higher education.

To change this educational context for a group of exceptional underprivileged students that, despite their hardships, managed to perform outstandingly in the Saber 11 test, the Colombian government implemented an intervention policy that ran between 2014 and 2018. For four years, 10,000 beneficiaries received a forgivable loan to enter the accredited higher education institution of their choice, for the duration of their studies. This demand-side subsidy included tuition fees and a stipend and was forgivable provided the student graduated. To qualify, students had to fulfill three requirements. First, they needed an exceptionally high score in the Saber 11 (top decile); second, their household needed to be categorized as extremely poor according to a state survey used to target social policy (SISBEN); and, finally, they had to be admitted by the program they applied to at an accredited higher education institution (Medina et al., 2018).

The program increased access to higher education for the target population by 46.5 percent (Londoño-Vélez, Rodríguez, & Sánchez, 2020) and disrupted the extreme patterns of class segregation, especially in Colombia's elite private universities where, for the first time, a high proportion of students did not belong to the most privileged classes. Most students chose private universities, mainly because of the institutions' perceived prestige. This makes sense in a very heterogeneous and unequal higher education system where labor market returns to education depend on the institution, with graduates from prestigious private universities having higher salaries (Barrera-Osorio & Bayona-Rodríguez, 2019). Others, despite wanting to enter a public university, did not pass the additional entrance exam. The private elite university in which we conducted our research is one of the most selective, prestigious, and expensive in Colombia, ranked among the top five in Latin America (Quacquarelli-Symonds, 2022). SPP dramatically changed its student composition (see Figure 1).

While the proportion of low socioeconomic status students (SES) was less than 7 percent the year before SPP started, it rose to about 25 percent of the incoming cohorts while the program lasted.[1] Thus, the program provided a unique opportunity to observe social mobility processes as they unfolded within an institution that due to the aforementioned signaling effects has better returns in the labor market. It also offered the possibility to observe how

[1] Percentages are for students from socioeconomic strata 1 and 2 (low SES), 3 and 4 (middle SES), and 5 and 6 (high SES). Strata is an official socioeconomic measure of the Colombian government as is explained in the methods section.

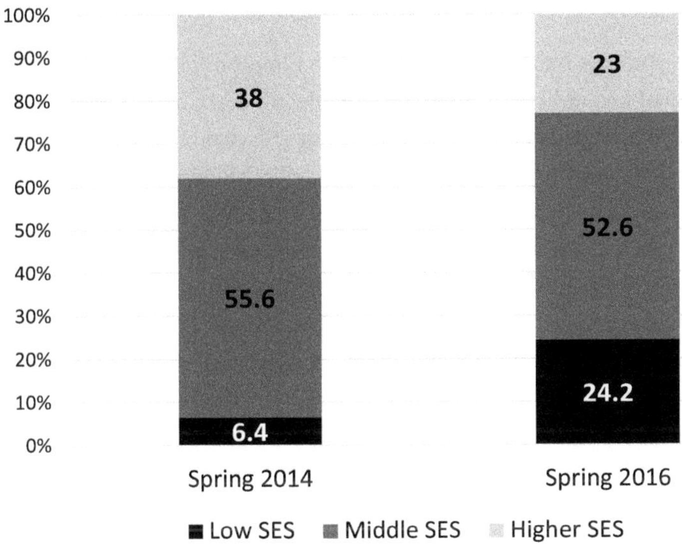

Figure 1 Study University incoming students' SES before and after the SPP program.

students from low SES backgrounds integrated into inter-class network formation, which is closely associated with increased social mobility opportunities. Finally, as an elite institution, the university also offered the possibility to investigate social closure, opportunity hoarding, and other mechanisms of social reproduction that tend to hinder social mobility.

1.4 The Study

This mixed-methods study was conducted over eight years at an elite higher education institution dubbed Study University. It involved various data collection methods, including network surveys, interviews, and ethnographic data.[2] Different types of data complement each other. The study began while individuals were still students, with the two-wave survey and the first wave of interviews taking place primarily between 2016 and 2017. Observations, follow-ups, and informal conversations were ongoing throughout the study. The second wave of interviews was held after the participants had graduated, in 2022. The sample was chosen to maximize variation with a particular focus on social class and academic majors.

[2] I also included five interviews with students on the SPP program from two other private universities and a public university, for an exploratory comparison with other contexts.

1.4.1 Participants

To categorize students into three socioeconomic groups or classes, we employed a combination of two indicators. First, we used the official Colombian division of households into six socioeconomic strata, which is based on place of residence and is commonly used as a proxy for class (Uribe Mallarino & Pardo Perez, 2006), and correlates with education and income. We integrated this with a relevant categorical variable in the context of this study, which is the participation in the SPP program, used to mark low socioeconomic status students and determine class relations in college. We considered all *becados* (scholarship students) as low SES students and also included the few students who, although not SPP scholarship recipients, lived in low-income areas of the city (strata 1 or 2).[3] Middle-class students were those who lived in strata 3 or 4 and were not SPP scholarship recipients. Upper-class or elite students were those who lived in strata 5 or 6. This division was consistent with other socioeconomic measures in our sample. While both middle-class and upper-class students typically had professional parents (but varying in their economic capital), low socioeconomic status students often had parents who had only completed secondary education. In this context, I use a variety of terms interchangeably to refer to the SPP recipients terms, including *becados* or *pilos* (the native categories), as well as "low SES," "underprivileged," "scholarship" or "lower-class students." Lower class translates to *clase baja* or "poor," which is how Colombians refer to those at the lower end of the socioeconomic spectrum. The term "working class" is not used in this context and is more associated to organized labor.

1.4.2 Ethnographic Data

Rather than separating ethnography from the other data, I conceived this research as a multi-method ethnography. I have been enmeshed in this program for eight years as a researcher, but I have also taken on the role of a participant observer. I have engaged with students by teaching them, offering counselling, observing their interactions, helping them find jobs, and sharing their challenges and triumphs. I have had the privilege of watching them grow. Besides my academic role, I have formulated concepts for university councils and other authorities, delivered presentations aimed at informing and influencing institutional practices, engaged in public debates about the program, written

[3] *SSP* students were living mostly in strata 1 or 2. However, a few that came from outside Bogotá were living with family members or in residences in higher-strata areas. Since they were categorized as poor to qualify for the scholarship based on their family background, we classify them within the lower socioeconomic group.

newspaper and academic articles and discussed them with participants and other audiences. I have also been involved in policy evaluation, conducted extensive reading on the subject, and endeavored to highlight both the program's successes and its challenges.

1.4.3 Survey Data

We collected individual and relational data in an online survey distributed through the institutional e-mail. Participants were students who started their undergraduate studies in January 2017. Responses were voluntary, and as an incentive, we raffled vouchers for a popular burger restaurant. Students completed the survey twice, a first wave toward the end of 2017, when they were finishing their first year, and a second wave toward the end of 2018, when they were finishing their second year at the university. The results presented in Section 3 pertain to this second wave (N = 149). Surveys included questions about their social connections, requiring students to identify, for all their classmates within their career cohort (we provided the names), whether they considered them as friends. These data allowed us to establish associations between nominations and relationships. We used these networks to analyze the extent of students' social integration in the university.

Surveys were administered in four different academic programs across diverse fields of study, which we do not disclose to protect confidentiality. These programs had a similar number of incoming students but different socioeconomic compositions. In particular, the proportion of scholarship students differed, resulting in diverse structures for potential interactions among students from different social classes and scholarship statuses (Neal, 2010). We compared the survey respondents to their entire cohorts on some variables and found no evidence of problematic trimming or biases. Respondents represented their cohorts in terms of sex, scholarship status, GPA and SES.

While I only briefly utilize these data in this Element, mainly in Section 3, they were crucial to demonstrating that lower-class students were not isolated or entirely segregated. On the contrary, they had several middle-class friends (a much more comprehensive analysis can be found in Álvarez-Rivadulla et al. [2022]).

1.4.4 Interviews

Table 1 summarizes the different stages of the interviews and includes detailed information about the sample. In the first wave of interviews (61), while interviewees where studying, some (34) interviews were conducted with a highly systematic quota sample. This sample was nested within the survey,

Table 1 Interview participants' demographics.

	Study 1	Labor market strict comparison	Longitudinal follow-up	Total
Sex distribution				
Male	38	20	11	
Female	23		9	
Class distribution				
Lower class	44	10	20	
Middle class	6			
Upper class	11	10		
Institution				
Study University	56	20	17	
Others	5		3	
Program				
Social Sciences	11		5	
Psychology	7		4	
Medicine	16		2	
Business	5		2	
Law	2	10	2	
Economics	14		5	
Engineering	5	10	2	
Literature	1		1	
Total *N* of interviews	**61**	**20**	**23**	**104**

selecting interviewees based on their network position (popular and isolated individuals from different SES for each program). Other interviews (27) were part of a less systematic sample and overrepresented the low SES population to gain a deeper understanding of their integration experience in college. These were not nested but aimed to maximize variation covering a wide range of programs and semesters.

Forty-three new interviews were conducted as a follow-up project to investigate the labor market. Twenty-three of them were part of a longitudinal follow-up of the initial interviews, aiming to track the progress of the interviewed students, including whether they had graduated or not, what happened to their college and other networks, and their post-graduation experiences, particularly focusing on the labor market. The remaining twenty interviews involved new subjects and were selected through a systematic sample from two different careers fields: law and computer engineering. These fields were chosen for their varying characteristics in terms of positions, salaries, and labor conditions, as well as the weight of the differing roles of social and cultural capital in their hiring processes. Following Rivera (2016), we selected privileged subjects – specifically, males pursuing privileged careers – for a more streamlined comparison. Our focus was on comparing *becados* with upper-class graduates (*Estrato* 6 only). This served as the foundation to the MA thesis of one my students and a co-authored paper (Pinzón Flechas & Alvarez-Rivadulla, 2023).

We analyzed transcriptions of interviews and field notes, with a focus on identifying recurring themes associated with students' trajectories and experiences in college and after graduation. The coding process used both theoretical and inductive strategies, allowing the incorporation of themes derived from existing literature as well as the emergence of new insights regarding the way class defines the college experience of working-class students. Theoretical codes included family and educational trajectories, cultural capital and its sub-codes, social capital, its sub-codes, etc. Codes that emerged from the data included shame, fear, pride, and other inequality and mobility-related emotions that we observed during fieldwork. Cases, coding, and analyses were discussed and triangulated in weekly team meetings, contributing to hypotheses-building and reliability.

1.4.5 Ethical Concerns

This project involved ethical challenges that went way beyond the IRB requirements (Blee & Currier, 2011). As a qualitative research team comprising university professors and students in the institution under study, our deep immersion in the research context yielded high-quality data but also raised a unique set of ethical concerns and responsibilities that extended beyond the formal research activities. Given the practical implications of our research for the students' well-being, and the personal relationships we built with them, we were involved in different interventions throughout the project. We presented ongoing results to relevant university authorities, students, and the community in general, to initiate conversations and inform policies on diversity. We also helped students that needed different forms of support, from counseling to collecting money to pay for tuition and connecting them with the university's psychological services. This implies that the end of this project is not clear; it continues to evolve. Even as I write these lines, I am arranging to meet with one of the students I have become close with who is coming to town and wants to update me on their progress and discuss a "personal and new" matter. I am also endorsing one of my former students and interviewees for a job opportunity as she is the most qualified candidate and in need of financial support. I am helping another student that found me through the internet, to see if she can secure a waiver from the Ministry of Education or the university so she can finish an extra-semester without having to pay. And I am preparing a presentation for the Academic Dean about the employability of our graduates. These are just some examples of the ethics of care that this project has entailed. More traditionally, we have used pseudonyms for the participants for narrative purposes, and to protect their identities.

1.5 A Note on Race

Although this study focuses on class, a note on race is important here, as most of the scholarship on school integration and diversity comes from the United States and focuses on racial disparities, but also because Latin American societies are deeply "pigmentocratic" (Telles, 2014), and Colombia is no exception (Urrea, Viáfara, & Viveros, 2014). Having darker skin and being racialized limits opportunities and social mobility (Viáfara López, 2017; Viveros Vigoya, 2022). A long history of colonization, slavery, and continuous institutional and everyday racism is behind current disparities in the educational attainment of indigenous peoples and blacks in the region and in Colombia in particular. It is precisely because of these deep inequalities that the scholarship students were of lighter skin than economically similar populations (Alvarez-Rivadulla, 2017). Those that were able to excel in their state exams despite being poor were not, in general, the darkest-skinned students in the country.

Although Study University does not collect data on ethnicity and race, the presence of Afro or indigenous students (and professors) is notably low. And darker skin students feel "othered," as the following reflections made by Josué, a Social Science student from the Caribbean Coast sharply testify. He wrote the following after discussing Du Bois in my undergraduate theory class.

> I am becoming blacker and blacker. For me, identity based on skin color was never very relevant. It seemed incomprehensible to me that in a multiethnic and multicultural region like the Caribbean, there could be such a thing as racism. However, when I arrived in Bogota and more precisely at this University, skin color and the identity built around it was one of the biggest shocks for me. Seeing so many people with the same skin tone [lighter] created a sense of chaos in my mind, I got frustrated, I simply could not believe it, I began to miss cultural diversity for the first time, especially in the university, because in the

> streets of southern Bogota (where I stay) and in the fantastic city center there was diversity and cultural richness, despite the ostentatious predominance of whiteness. (. . .) When I started to interact in the university, both with students and professors, most of the time the topic of race, racism, exclusion, and marginalization were discussed in my presence. The truth is that I have always liked to explore and understand these issues in order to put an end to them, but I think it is a bit annoying that (at least at the beginning of my relationships) they always talked about the same thing with me. What frustrated me even more was the awkwardness I perceived from them when discussing this topic. They would avoid eye contact, or when they did look at me, they would do so without blinking. It continues to strike me as peculiar how many people at Study University confidently discuss an object of study, but when they come into contact with that object, they hesitate and even become elusive and indifferent. This makes me think that their discourse is reserved only for the halls and auditoriums of the Study University and not for reality.
>
> I didn't realize it at first, but in time and more precisely when they began to call me *moreno* and to look at me when they talked about black culture and its dances such as the *mapale*, that they associated me with the black identity. But this constructed identity of the black from the center of the country can be an interesting subject of research. I think that at Study University, the idea of blackness goes beyond skin color, that is, there are some attributes that socially shape your image. I am not only black at the University because of my brown or *trigueño* skin color, but also because I don't pronounce my Ss, because I carry my lunch in a Tupperware [coca], because I did not study in a bilingual school or because I did not read Foucault in the last year of high school, or because I have a scholarship and I am a foreigner, etc. This clash has brought up a lot of feelings and internal debates. They make me question and rethink how I am socially categorized under a specific group or about what to identify myself with, and the most difficult thing is that I am not part of, nor do I have the power to challenge that political power that categorizes me, that constructs a portrait by which I must identify myself and by which others identify me in the social space.

Josué painfully and clearly reveals how race and otherness mark him in this new white elite context. He illustrates how interpretations of racial categories intersect with class in mestizo societies like the Colombian one, where a higher social class can lighten your skin in the eyes of others, and there's a perceived obligation to whiten when upwardly mobile as shown by Viveros Vigoya (2022). As interesting as this is, I did not encounter enough cases in the interviews to thoroughly analyze the additional impact of racialization on hindering social mobility.

1.6 A Note on Gender

As necessary as a reflection on race is, of course, a reflection on gender. The literature has emphasized the role of gender in social mobility, typically negatively affecting women and sexual minorities. Disparities in educational attainment and choices, occupational segregation, the gender wage gap, unpaid care work, maternity penalties, the glass ceiling in higher-ranking professions, open and covert discrimination, and other factors undermine women's possibilities for upward mobility. Like in many countries, despite the remarkable improvement in female labor market participation and education in the last decades, a sizeable gender gap still exists in Colombia. This gap is not explained by women's characteristics but by labor market differential returns (Badel & Peña, 2010). Women have surpassed men in tertiary education, for example. Yet, they face a glass ceiling effect and "quicksand floor effect," representing differential labor market returns for women both at the top and at the bottom of the distribution.

According to the available national data on the SPP program, "females disproportionately benefit from financial aid in accessing and graduating from high-quality colleges. However, females experience similar learning and earnings gains to males since they are less likely to graduate from STEM degrees and more likely to graduate from social sciences and humanities" (Londoño-Vélez, Rodríguez, Sánchez, & Álvarez-Rivadulla, 2022, p. 24). Thus, women's greater achievements in accessing and graduating end up leveling up in the labor market because of the unequal sexual division of disciplines and associated labor markets.

During fieldwork, I continuously paid attention to gender differences in social integration to the university and in labor market trajectories. While I did not find clear gender differences in number or types of friends, as developed later in the text, I did find more demands in terms of aesthetics for women to belong to the expected profile of an elite college student. Yet, these demands were not completely clear. Rather than having a defined dress code, the environment of this college resembled what Friedman and Laurison (2019, p. 25) refer to as "studied informality," characterized by casual modes of self-presentation in dressing and interaction that follow complex, but informal, codes. Thus, simple rules like associating price with style, or preferring high culture, are insufficient to make adequate choices in terms of cultural capital (Corredor & Álvarez Rivadulla, 2024).

This can make camouflaging easier or cheaper, but at the same time, more complicated because the rules are not clear. Mentions about having to straighten their hair appeared only among either women or, in one case, in an interview with a gay male student. Straight hair is often perceived a racial identifier, associated with whiteness and cultural conformity in many Latin American contexts, particularly evident in Colombia. In contrast, curly or wavy hair is either curly subject to racialization or viewed as unkempt (Rodríguez & Archer, 2022). Apprehension regarding clothing choices, especially during the first semester, emerged predominantly among women. However, I lack systematic evidence of other gender-based distinctions during college, unlike findings in similar contexts such as the Chilean one (Rodríguez Anaiz, 2023). Post-college, in job interviews, some women conveyed experiencing remarks about appearing "too young," for their positions, that they had to wear makeup and dress differently to look more professional. Male young professionals did not mention receiving similar comments.

Where I did find clearer gender disparities was in the caregiving workload, especially post-college. As detailed in Section 4, many scholarship graduates assume the role of primary providers of their families. However, women, in addition to their economic responsibilities, have to take on more caregiving duties in their households. This includes helping to raise siblings, directly caring for their mothers or grandmothers, and so on. Despite the absence of significant differences in average earnings between females and males based on general quantitative data, I contend that any comparison must consider nonpaid working hours. This perspective is crucial for understanding the potential impact on paid labor, social mobility, and general well-being as individuals progress through life.

Finally, as expounded in Section 2, the role of women, especially mothers, is pivotal in the social mobility of their offspring. Quantitative studies have consistently indicated that the influence of maternal education on children's educational attainment tends to surpass that of paternal education. Moreover, qualitatively, it is evident that the role of women is very important in the intergenerational transmission of class and mobility expectations (Vigoya & Hernández, 2010).

2 Before the Opportunity: Mothers and Teachers behind Academic Outliers

Sergio remembers his elementary school teacher as someone crucial to his academic success. John, his professor in a rural area in Colombia's Caribbean coast, invited him to participate in the United Nations academic simulation model, in which Sergio assumed the role of the president of Israel and other countries. He remembers that he created a video for a project with John, which garnered him a prize.

> That project helped me . . . helped me to wake up and realize that studying is the pathway to progress. I had to assume the role of president. And then all that motivation, I saw my surroundings on the one hand, and I saw the possibilities that would open up through studying on the other. Let's start studying hard, I thought. And study is what I did.

I met Sergio in one of my classes. He was enthusiastic, opinionated, and thoughtful. When I learned he was a scholarship student, I decided to interview him. Although we had several informal conversations before, we did the formal interview online. He showed me his room at an aunt's house in Bogotá, where he was staying, given that he had traveled very far to study. The room was full of framed diplomas from his multiple prizes with the UN model and other academic achievements. He was very proud of them. And he had reasons to be proud. His background is extremely deprived, and he is a complete outlier in his family and community. His was one of the harsher stories to hear. Abandoned by his mom at an early age, he was raised by a step-grandma together with his brothers. He remembers being hungry and malnourished at an early age, but later, when grandma became the primary caregiver, things got better. They still lacked a lot of basic needs, but grandma brought discipline to their lives. A very religious woman, she was very strict with homework times, daily routines, the way they dressed, and their hair styles. She managed to raise Sergio and his three younger brothers on her miserable informal salary for cleaning a local school.

Sergio's story shows the black box of academic outliers like him. Caregivers, usually women, usually mothers but also grandmothers (or a step grandmother as in this case) were pivotal in many stories. And professors were as well. We know parental education is a strong predictor of children's education. We also know that different social classes raise their kids differently. Yet, there is still a lot we do not know in terms of explaining those cases that are not easily explained by the regular theories surrounding social mobility. Indeed, the stories in this Element challenge our understandings. Most parents did not reach tertiary education. Some did. But Sergio's story of an uneducated domestic worker raising an academically successful and persistent student was not unique. There were several stories of uneducated mothers or grandmothers who have great expectations of mobility for their children or grandchildren. The existence of these outliers stems, at least in part, from those expectations, paired with household routines and other nurturing practices that helped students value education and aspire to do well. Certainly, there might be other factors contributing to the success of *pilos*. Yet, the narratives I collected consistently highlighted the role of mothers or other women caregivers as influential figures and sources of inspiration for these youngsters.

This section investigates the factors behind exceptional youngsters that become statistical outliers with outstanding academic abilities despite their poverty. The exploration navigates the historical process of habitus development where, as Crozier, Reay, and Clayton (2019, p. 925) state, "there must have already been something in these students' habitus which has enabled them to transcend fields – from the non-university to the university context." The analysis centers on the role of the two main institutions which determine life opportunities: family and schools. In so doing, it unveils the role played by mothers and teachers, particularly their expectations of social mobility for those youngsters. Theoretical discussions are rooted in the sociology of class reproduction and address some of its pitfalls.

2.1 Families, Mothers, and Expectations

A family's socioeconomic background is a strong predictor of academic achievement. This effect tends to be stronger in societies with low social mobility. Besides access to better resources, from nutrition to education, we know that everyday socialization practices also influence class transmission, mainly through the acquisition of different forms of cultural capital. Cultural capital, a concept developed by Pierre Bourdieu (Bourdieu, 1984, 2018), refers to "the symbols, ideas, tastes, and preferences that can be strategically used as resources in social action" (Scott & Marshall, 2009), in particular for status distinction, opportunity hoarding, exclusion, and other forms of class reproduction or mobility.

Lareau's (2011) pioneering work in sociology revealed that middle-class families transmit middle-class cultural capital and aspirations through upbringing. In her interviews and ethnographic observations of family nurturing and caring priorities and practices, she saw that the working class and the middle class had very different parenting styles. Middle-class families took their children to several extracurricular activities, leaving them with little free time. They also emphasized the use of language, conversation, and negotiated rules, which fostered a sense of empowerment among their children. This "concerted cultivation" creates adults who do well in school, know how to talk and challenge authority, and are good at managing time, qualities needed to remain in the middle class. Lower-class parents, in turn, gave more autonomy to their children, offering them more free time and taking them to fewer or no structured activities. These children were able to play and watch TV with friends in their neighborhoods or extended families. Rules were stricter and nonnegotiable, and adults used more physical forms of discipline. This "natural growth" parenting style generates students and later adults who are less able to challenge authority and negotiate rules. Either they accept or withdraw. They also have more difficulty navigating middle-class institutions such as college if they manage to enter.

Interviews with SPP students explored parenting styles and childhood experiences through different questions. Interestingly, they did not match what Lareau found for working-class families. On the one hand, although one of the criteria for obtaining the scholarship was being socioeconomically deprived, families were heterogeneous in their cultural capital. Although most parents had only finished primary education, a few had started or even finished university studies, not in the best universities, but they had professional degrees, nonetheless. Those students' good results are less of a surprise. Their parents' own aspirations and cultural capital led them to do well at school. On the other hand, and perhaps more interestingly, parents, especially mothers, with limited formal education, were still a great source of cultural capital for their children in ways that helped them have a positive educational experience. The role of mothers as the main channels of cultural capital because of the unequal division of care labor has been highlighted in different studies (Reay, 2000). However, in this case, the significance of mothers is magnified by the fact that many *becados* come from households led by single mothers.

Thus, mothers' own mobility aspirations, albeit their profound lack of opportunities, impacted their children's. They took them to extracurricular activities such as church choir or various sports; they supervised homework or simply encouraged them to keep studying more than they had the chance to. For example, Luis, a black student with astoundingly good grades, two majors, and an impossibly tight schedule, is a first-generation student as well as a scholarship holder. His father did not finish elementary school, and his mother only received her high school degree several months after Luis interview. She still managed to raise him in such a way that he never doubted he would go on to get a higher education. He stated the following in this respect:

> I'd always wanted to go to college, and I always thought like, well, there has to be some other way of getting into college. If we don't have the money, I don't know, something's got to happen. So, when they launched SPP, that was an excellent opportunity. With my score [on the national standardized test], well I was beyond happy (. . .). I think I was influenced by my mother. As I was telling you, she always wants to move forward, to better herself. So ever since I was little, I knew that I had to do the best that I could. I didn't know what I wanted to study, I'm not one of those "I always wanted to be a doctor" people. But I did want to study something, and to be excellent at whatever I did (. . .). During junior year, medicine caught my attention. My mom bought me a book with botanic, zoology and anatomy stuff, and I liked the anatomy part (. . .). I've loved it so far; I don't regret a thing.

For Luis, the pivotal factor in his success was the high expectations his mother always held for him, as well as her efforts to provide the cultural capital she lacked (for example, by buying him books, a commodity which not many low-income families can afford). Most cases revealed more features of concerted cultivation than of natural growth. Scholarship students participated in various extracurricular activities, reflecting a deliberate effort to enrich their experiences. Although many used to have free time playing outside, especially those that lived in smaller cities or towns, several parents did not allow them to play outside because they saw the neighborhood as a risk and a bad influence. These parents wanted their children to be different; they wanted them to be able to get out of the neighborhood. Taking them to extracurricular activities was a way to keep them busy and not outside. Valentina, a cultural studies student, was an example of this:

- Well yes, my mommy, has always been very hard on me, very strict, but more like in terms of behavior, not academically, but I always saw that they were studying [parents and brother] so I always thought, "I want to be like them."

- **Did you do any other hobbies when you were little? You mentioned skating. Who took you to skating?**

- Well, I did a lot of things when I was little, like my mom wanted to keep me busy in the afternoons, so first, she enrolled me in some art courses. Then, she tried to get me into a music thing, but I dropped out because I didn't like to sing, because I thought I could not really sing well. Next, they put me in figure skating, and I didn't like it, and well, my dad, took me skating once and I liked it a lot, and I was about 10 years old and then I started skating and well, my dad, he saw that I was doing well, and he changed me to a better school. (. . .) I trained every day except Sundays, from 3 to 6, and I also went up to Monserrate [a city mountain with a trail] every Saturday. I used to love doing that, and my parents would use it to punished me, so if I misbehaved or talked back they wouldn't let me train, and that was the worst for me.

Although mothers appeared more, in part because fathers were not there in many cases, Valentina's case shows a similar mechanism but with her father. He always motivated her to study because he had wanted to study and could not afford it, despite getting the best score in his standardized exam when finishing high school in the whole of the Boyacá department. He got a partial scholarship, but he couldn't afford the other half to continue studying. He wanted to be an engineer, but he ended up working first as a driver for many years, and later, after taking a few business administration course, doing accounting work for some businesses. When asked who she admired the most, Valentina immediately mentioned him.

> Well, my dad. Because even though he couldn't, that is, it makes me very angry that he couldn't study because he really is very *pilo*. I mean, he always had the best grades, he always excelled in everything, it makes me really angry that he couldn't have an opportunity like the one I had. You see? (. . .) And despite that, he went ahead, and well, right now he's fine.

Based on the interviews with these academic outliers, I can say that they were generally raised with significant adult involvement, that many of them went to extracurricular activities, and that women caregivers, particularly mothers, but also grandmothers, were crucial for their academic success. This crucial role was not mostly through involvement with school tasks or overseeing all of their children's free time, like in Lareau's (2011) description of US middle-class families. Instead, these women served as exemplars of resilience and strongly believed in the importance of education to their children for social mobility and personal success in life.

There are no similar studies for different types of families or youth in Colombia, so we do not know to what extent these parenting approaches are generalizable among the lower classes.

Yet, what we do know is that Colombians tend to be optimistic about future mobility, regardless of their income, and despite being pessimistic (and realistic) when evaluating their previous mobility experiences. They believe their children will do better than they did (Londoño-Vélez, 2011). Colombians also tend to see education as a crucial mechanism to become and remain middle class (Álvarez-Rivadulla, 2023). Even some of those growing up in the poorest neighborhoods and with no role models in their families or surroundings aspire to study after high school, although most of them either do not in the end or drop out soon after starting (Díaz Vargas, 2013). Despite the fact that many share mobility aspirations in Colombia, what may distinguish high achievers like the SPP recipients is the transmission not only of mobility aspirations but also of specific skills to perform well in the system and persist in their goals.

2.2 Exceptional Teachers in Underprivileged Institutions

In the context of the educational class apartheid (García-Villegas & López, 2011) in Colombia, as outlined earlier, particularly the divide between public and private education (within the public system as well), it is not surprising that the majority of scholarship students came from underfunded state schools. Most interviewees remember their high school as academically challenging environments with prevalent social issues. However, many of them describe having found, in these very schools, a teacher who played a pivotal role in changing the trajectory of their lives.

Valeria, a literature student, who had great academic and social difficulties when entering college and had to drop out for a semester, study English to survive in college, and come back, described her high school as having been very problematic.

> We missed a lot of classes, [the teachers] didn't have good teaching methods. For example, the Physics teacher, no lie, she never explained a thing, she

> always just gave us activities to do on our own (. . .). Instead of having class, we would watch movies, so we learned no physics or chemistry whatsoever.

Socially, Valeria said the school had a "heavy atmosphere" because of the students and the neighborhood. She said that in her school:

> There was a lot of drug abuse, there's always been like gang fights in the area, that sort of thing (. . .). We had much older classmates, I don't even know how old some of them were, and by middle school they were already pregnant. About three of them had kids before finishing school.

This school environment, which is the norm rather than the exception in several low-income neighborhoods, presents huge academic, social, cultural, and emotional disadvantages for its students. Yet, even in those educational environments, most interviewees told stories of finding one teacher, generally a social sciences' teacher, that showed them a way out. They remembered teachers that were dedicated, that gave them some key career information, and teachers who showed them they were good and could do better.

We have already seen the power of some teachers in the case of Sergio in the opening part of this section. Carolina tells a similar story. Her state school in a working-class neighborhood in Bogotá (Patio Bonito) was a huge. She recalls that many of the teachers left students that "didn't want to learn" outside and only taught the ones that did. Carolina found a particularly inspiring group of teachers there that talked to the students as equals, giving her recognition and motivation. She particularly remembers her math teacher, a highly qualified teacher who started sending Carolina to Math Olympics once she realized how good she was. With them, she felt singled out in the multitude, listened to, and promoted as a good student.

> There were two teachers to whom I still say that I owe them my Saber 11 [end of high school standardized exam], the math teacher, who was very good, (. . .), she was tough, she was still studying her doctorate at that time and she was very understanding and saw that I liked mathematics, so I started to go to Olympiads (. . .). And Ángela also, the Spanish teacher, I didn't have such a good relationship with her because I didn't like her very much, but she was very conversational. At my school, I think we used to take advantage of the spaces between classes to talk about interesting things. I think that is so valuable, that they could have conversations with 12, 15, maximum 16 year-old children, about politics, because their opinion seemed valid to them. Or about abortion, there was a debate that day in the classroom and well, we didn't have class, but we learned something, to debate, at least, to listen. So, things like that, and they had strategies like that. For example, in Spanish, it was like "let's set a goal of a number of books we are going to read. Everyone chose a book." And I read many books. I remember I got to eighth grade with

> the book *Satanás* by Mario Mendoza (laughs) [it's a book about a massive murder in Bogotá]. I arrived another day with *Memorias de mis putas tristes* [by García Marquez, also perhaps for older kids]. And she was like: "Carolina, thank you for reading that." Yes, it was the book that each of us liked. So, today I also appreciate that, like that treatment that they gave us.

Carolina mentioned feeling challenged academically by these two teachers but also mentioned many noncognitive factors she valued from her school, and that she felt were important for who she is now, a critical woman, who has finished her psychology degree. She also remembered a professor that helped her choose which university to go to when she won the scholarship. He had information that nobody else in her environment had. His children were studying at a private university and he told Carolina that if she could choose, she should choose Study University, because he thought that even though it was more elitist, there was less risk of being discriminated against. She still likes to go back to her high school. Teachers invite her to tell her story to new students, as a role model, which makes her feel valued and useful.

Stories like Carolina's or Sergio's, of good experiences with exceptional teachers in underprivileged institutions, were common in many of the children's narratives. This stands in contrasts with Jack's (2019) finding for the US context, where he identified a group of "privileged poor" Afro kids receiving scholarships to attend elite high schools. These youngsters learned early on in life how to behave in middle- and upper-class institutions and how to manage inter-class relations. These youngsters overwhelmingly secured scholarships for prestigious colleges and, in contrast to their counterparts that did not have similar experiences, excelled in these academic settings. While I did find some very rare instances of "privileged poor," who had had similar experiences in private high schools, the majority did not fit the "privileged poor" characterization as outlined by Jack. Instead, they were students who had the fortune of encountering good teachers in underprivileged schools. This underscores the significant influence teachers wield in altering academic trajectories even in adverse conditions.

2.3 Conclusion: The Power of Opportunity

SPP students and upwardly mobile students in general are exceptional. We know little about exceptional success stories in breaking the barriers of social reproduction (Streib, 2017). While conventional wisdom tends to attribute individual effort to all cases of mobility, sociological perspectives often reveal a broader pattern: those who were previously privileged tend to sustain or augment their advantage, even when effort is taken into account. However, socially mobility does occur, albeit infrequently.

Psychology, on the other hand, introduces individual explanations such as grit or personality traits to better explain the variation among those who, without prior privilege, manage to thrive. The students in this study exhibit exceptional qualities on a personal level. Listening to their narratives and seeing them overcome challenges over the years, it is evident that they are clearly resilient and resourceful. Yet, from a sociological perspective, I have tried to understand common factors in their trajectories that could help, at least in part, explain why those features emerged.

There are methodological restrictions to any generalization here, as I do not have a control group of similar socioeconomically deprived youngsters with lower educational outcomes. Despite these limitations, recurring themes in the stories, such as parents – particularly mothers – holding expectations of social mobility via education, and the influence of exceptional teachers demonstrating a different trajectory was possible, are prevalent enough to allow me to conclude that they likely played a substantial role in explaining these students' exceptional academic records.

Yet, it is important to point out that these features might not have been relevant enough had it not been for the opening of an opportunity. Without the SPP program, these exceptional youngsters would not be where they are now, particularly given the current conditions of higher education in Colombia. The first impact evaluation of the program is clear in finding that they would not have been able to access higher education in top-quality institutions. The second impact evaluation is clear in revealing that they would not have graduated at the same speed nor would they have achieved comparable positions or salaries without the program's influence (Londoño-Vélez et al., 2022).

The siblings of these scholarship students were not able to enjoy the same opportunities. They too tend to want to study or are studying but their trajectories are harsher. Sergio's brother, for example, who he considers to be much smarter than himself, would like to study industrial engineering but is currently working at a greengrocery in his town and living with their grandma hoping to be able to study one day. His state exam results were not high enough for him to be granted a full scholarship, and even if he goes to a public university, he still must pay some level of fees and be able to survive financially in the closest city, Barranquilla, where they do not have any relatives. The most important lesson from this policy experiment is the transformative power of opening doors previously closed to a group of 40,000 students, enabling them to thrive. It's essential not to lose sight of the broader impact – the forest – while trying to explain variation within specific trees.

3 Entering an Elite College: The Relational Costs and Work of Building Social Capital [4]

Previous studies have shown that less privileged students who attend elite colleges do not only have to master challenging academic content but also have to learn about elite manners, how to speak to professors, how to behave, and the rules of the game in terms of gaining credentials, knowledge, or wealth (Aries, 2008; Armstrong & Hamilton, 2013; Corredor et al., 2020a; Jack, 2016; Khan, 2011; Lee, 2016; Lee & Kramer, 2013; Stuber, 2011). They may suffer from more or less direct forms of classism and exclusion (Ferguson & Lareau, 2018), simply feel estranged in an unfamiliar environment, or overwhelmed by the additional effort needed to fit in. They may feel torn between two worlds, that of home and that of school, developing what Friedman (2016), recovering Bourdieu's (1998, 2007) own personal experience and that of other upwardly mobile in elite schools dubbed a divided, *clivé* or *clift* habitus.

While the associated costs and apprehensions may lead to isolation and, consequently, low performance and diminished subjective well-being, as it does in other contexts (Robbins et al., 2004; Rubin, Evans, & Wilkinson, 2016), this was not the case for the majority of the *pilos*. Rather than isolating themselves or resorting to safe homophilic relations, they confronted the challenges of their new elite environment by establishing connections with more affluent students. In so doing, they navigated the concealed relational costs of forming friendships with students from more privileged backgrounds. This involved overcoming fears and experiences of discrimination and microaggressions, as well as confronting barriers related to cultural and economic capital. They employed strategies such as camouflaging or disclosure and, at times, adopted culturally and socially omnivorous approaches. These social costs and this relational work (Zelizer, 2012) were more challenging in more elite environments than in more diverse settings. It was, however, in these elite environments that the most interesting, potentially useful (Chetty et al., 2022), and unexpected encounters occurred.

For many of our interviewees from low socioeconomic backgrounds at Study University, making friends was at first perceived as a challenge. This contrasted with the experience of many privileged students, particularly those from elite schools, who had the advantage of pre-existing connections with fellow students from shared educational backgrounds, elite social clubs, or other social

[4] Most of this section appeared before in this article: Álvarez-Rivadulla, Camelo, Vargas-Serani, and Viáfara (2023). The relational costs of crossing class lines. *The British Journal of Sociology*. The graphs appeared before in this other article: Álvarez-Rivadulla, Jaramillo, Fajardo, Cely, Molano, and Montes (2022). College integration and social class. Higher Education, 84(3), 647–669.

spaces. This pre-established familiarity made it easier for them to relate and adapt seamlessly to university life. Camila, a lower-income student, recounts her experience after initially attending college:

> When I started college, I felt lonely. At first, I felt like I didn't have any friends, so I'd tell my mom that I was going to be alone all my life in college and that it was ugly, and sometimes I cried about it.

Camila's experience and feelings of loneliness and related anxiety resonate with those of other students who often recalled the challenges of initiating conversations and forming connections. It was not solely about arriving alone, given that they were exceptional among their school friends and context; they also feared discrimination as outsiders in the elite university environment.

These students recalled being overly conscious about personal appearance, buying clothes they thought were appropriate for the new environment, feeling inadequate, and going home crying after orientation events because they hadn't talked to anyone. Some even thought of dropping out. However, they persisted. Luckily, for the average scholarship student, their extra effort paid off. On average, and contrary to the literature that predicts their isolation, scholarship students were as popular as other types of classmates by their second semester. This observation aligns with both the findings of this qualitative fieldwork and other more quantitative network study (Álvarez-Rivadulla et al., 2022). Cases of isolation were very rare. Through opportunities for interaction and relational work, they not only made friends but, more importantly for this study, formed cross-class school relations and, in some instances, developed close friendships.

How do low socioeconomic status students navigate cross-class interactions in extremely unequal contexts? Previous research has described the high costs of college integration for underprivileged students, which, in turn, negatively impact academic performance and general well-being. These studies tend to concentrate on cultural capital costs, such as catching up with assumed middle-class or elite capital and dealing with two worlds. Less has been said about the related, yet specific, social capital costs, the costs of making friends, especially more privileged friends, and the strategies or relational work used to overcome them.

The concept of relational work is useful to illuminate what it takes to build social capital. According to Zelizer (2012, p. 149), relational work is "the creative effort people make establishing, maintaining, negotiating, transforming, and terminating interpersonal relations." The idea that building social capital takes work is already mentioned in Bourdieu (2018) when he defines it and speaks of the "investment strategies" behind potentially useful relationships. Relational work across classes, what Gray and Kish-Gephart (2013) have dubbed "class work," brings additional anxieties and challenges. Social capital

Table 2 Lower-class students' relations in college, by type, associated costs, benefits, and required class relational work.

Type of relations	Costs	Benefits	Class relational work
Isolation	Low academic achievement and subjective well-being.	None.	Evasion
Homophilic relations	Not identified in this research. Perhaps fear of being stigmatized or not moving up.	Safety. Shared understandings/ Identification.	Overcoming the first stage of not knowing anybody.
Heterophilic relations	Gaps in cultural capital and economic conditions. Fear and experiences of micro-aggressions/ discrimination.	Belonging to the institution and to middle classness. Expansion of cultural capital and future expectations (both important for upward mobility).	Camouflaging Disclosure Omnivorousness

does not emerge just because of mixing and contact as many social policies assume. Relational work is needed.

Table 2 summarizes the different types of relationships that lower-class students engaged in during college, their differential costs and benefits, and the relational work strategies they used. This section describes and analyzes those associated with building up cross-class ties amid deep inequality: camouflaging, disclosure, and adopting socially and culturally omnivorous approaches.

3.1 Building Networks

Contrary to the literature predicting isolation for those who feel like outsiders in college, a network survey encompassing students of four different majors[5] revealed no statistically significant differences in the reported number of friends based on social class (Figure 2). This measurement considered both the number

[5] See the methods section for details on the survey.

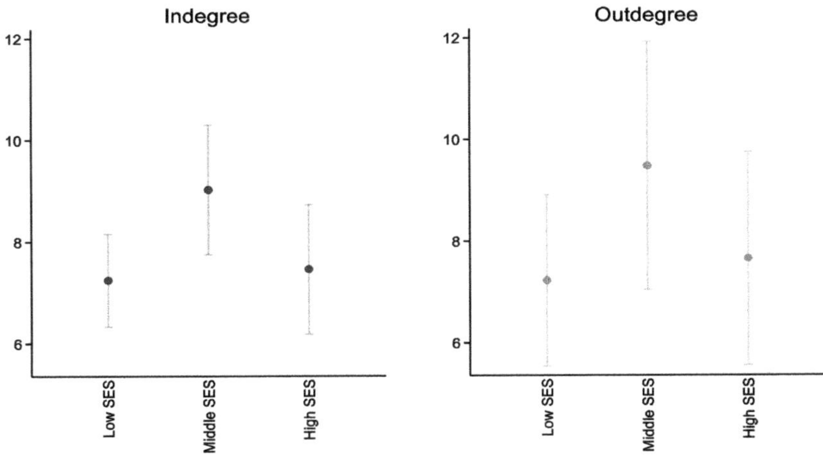

Figure 2 Average number of incoming nominations as a friend (indegree) and outgoing nominations (outdegree) by SES, with confidence intervals.

of classmates nominating a certain student as their friend (indegree) and the number of friends that student, in turn, nominates as her friends (outdegree). On average, lower-class students reported having as many friends as their middle-class and upper-class counterparts (about 7 to 9 friends in their cohort).

Figure 3 further demonstrates that, as expected, low SES students tend to have more friends with a similar SES, but cross-class friendships are not uncommon. Although less likely with high-SES classmates, such friendships exist (on average, each low SES has one high-SES friend). Moreover, cross-class friendships are even more common with middle-SES classmates. In fact, middle-SES students seem to act as brokers in these networks, connecting with both low- and high-SES classmates.

While friendships with other scholarship students gave lower-class students a safe environment with shared experiences and cultural capital, and the same economic restrictions, friendships with higher-class students gave them the opportunity to gain cultural capital, diversify experiences, and a foster sense of belonging to the institution and to the new class environment. A business administration student with two close friends, a middle-class one, and another scholarship student, explains what she gains from homophilic relationships:

> Do you agree with the statement made by a scholarship student: "the scholarship students with the scholarship students and the rich with the rich"?
> Well, I find it extremely hateful because, I mean, even though it's horrible to say it, we feel more identified with each other among *becados*. There is more

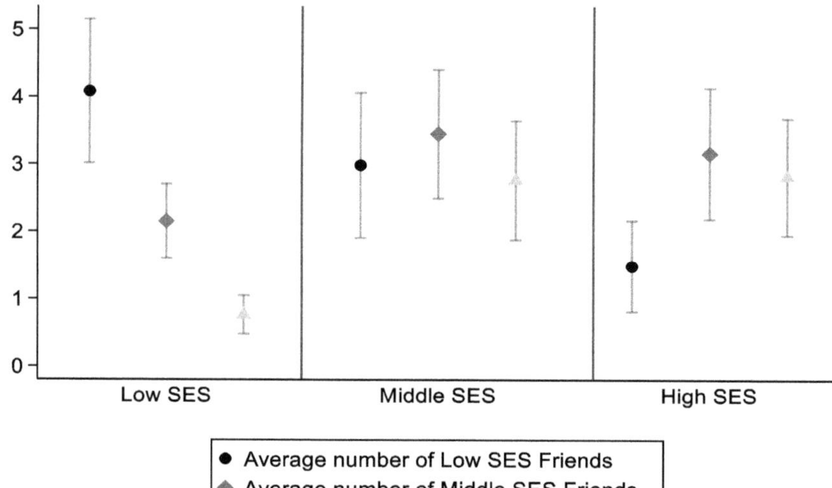

Figure 3 Average number of different SES friends (outdegree) by students' SES.

> "feeling." But that doesn't mean that I can't be friends with someone who is not a scholarship student. I mean, Verónica, for example, is the closest person to me at the university and she's not a scholarship recipient and she knows perfectly well that I am. I don't have to lie to her, I mean, no. So, you can't generalize. It's just normal that we look for each other among *becados* (. . .). Like, for example, when I find out that there is someone who lives near my neighborhood it's great, because here they all live in the North. But that doesn't mean I can't be friends with someone who lives up North!!!

Throughout the interview, she also shows what she has gained from more heterophilic relationships. She has felt welcomed by most classmates. She feels she belongs to the university and her expectations about the future have changed.

> The first day, they put us all in a huge auditorium and there were about 80 people. I felt that everyone knew everyone, and that I was the only stranger. It looked like they all came from the same school, all from *Los Nogales* [one of the most elite schools in the city] (laughs), except from me. (. . .) It was difficult, I felt strange. Well, I mean, thank God everything went well, I met very nice people. In the first semester the university was overly cooperative with us, they spoiled us a lot (. . .) I don't have a single complaint. It was a very good experience. Obviously, I had to adapt to the transition from school to university, like anyone else. But, really, I can't tell you that I felt different because I had a scholarship. No, I didn't.
>
> (. . .)

> The university opens doors and allows you to see things that you didn't see before. So, for example, I've always been drawn to the business field, and, among my distant aspirations, I wanted to be an entrepreneur. I wanted to have my own company, but it was such a far-off dream. I mean, it's difficult. I would have been happy with just a job that I could support myself with. Right now, it clearly isn't, *my aspirations have totally changed.* I want to be a businesswoman, and *not just any businesswoman,* I want to be *a successful businesswoman.* (...) Yes, the aspirations, the people that you meet. That's it, you meet a lot of people there [at university]. I mean, obviously there are all kinds of people, like anywhere else, but there are a lot of very educated people, with many aspirations that also motivate you to progress.

The meaning of a close friendship, generally understood by students of all social classes, inevitably involved more than just sharing schoolwork – it encompassed shared free time activities, mutual trust, support, and intimacy. For lower-class students this was much easier, effortless, and more immediate with other lower-class students. These relationships were characterized by a sense of commonality, from language to humor to past high school experiences, not to mention the same economic restrictions or proximity in nearby neighborhoods.

Lower-class students tended to describe conversations with higher-class friends as more "academic," "rational," circumscribed to the university. Yet, half of our forty-four lower-class interviewees mentioned at least one higher-class friend among their three closest university friends. Most of these friends were middle class as determined through various class indicators gathered in the interviews. These indicators included not being on an SPP scholarship, attending a private (though not elite) high school, having professional parents, or living in a middle-class neighborhood). In some cases, data triangulation was possible (e.g., when we had those friends in our data, we could check which official strata they lived in, with strata 3 or 4 indicating that they were middle class). Some were identified as upper middle class, but only exceptionally as upper class. We identified the latter mainly because they went to international bilingual schools.

3.2 Relational Costs in Cross-Class Relations

3.2.1 Fear and Experiences of Micro-aggressions/Discrimination

If making friends in general was challenging for the underprivileged students at the beginning of their university experience, crossing class lines to make friends was even more demanding. The already mentioned fears of discrimination were heightened with actual experiences of class-based micro-aggressions in the form of jokes or overheard comments.

The case of Carolyn, a scholarship student, illustrates micro-aggression or covert discrimination between classes. She expressed this experience passionately and with great anger during a class discussion on university inequality. Carolyn spoke about the hypocrisy she personally encountered among elite students. In the unequal and segregated city of Bogotá, students not only live in different neighborhoods, but they also use different means of transportation. Scholarship students often rely on public transportation, heading toward the working-class neighborhoods in the South of Bogotá. On the other hand, more affluent students have a car-pooling system, called "Wheels," exclusively serving the North and the West of the city. Carolyn shared an incident when she used Wheels to visit a friend in the North.

> I believe that there is significant discrimination, but people refrain from expressing it because they are afraid that they will be criticized. I want to share an experience from my first semester. (. . .) The only person who really knew me was the driver. The others were classmates but I didn't know them well. They start talking in the back of the car: 'Some *pilos* show that they really are *pilos*. There are people who, you don't want to say anything, but you can tell that they shouldn't be here, judging by how they dress . . . With some people you can tell they don't look like us.' Well, actually you can't because I'm also a *pilo*, *pendeja*! (asshole). So, when I got out of the car, I asked my friend to please tell them I was a *pilo* and, hopefully, they'll be ashamed of what they said. These are comments they feel comfortable making in what they perceive as a safe space.

Although Carolyn feels privileged among *pilos* due to her parents' investment in her education despite not having an education themselves, and even though she has a diversified network of friends and feels well integrated into the university, she still occasionally encounters these comments. Even if they are infrequent, instances of classism make her angry and serve as a reminder that she is considered an outsider by some.

The same happened to Zharik, who was dating an upper-class peer. Although Zharik is a very class-proud student that feels that she deserves to be where she is because of her achievements, she too has been subject to classism. Like many other scholarship students, she feared discrimination when she came from her hometown to Bogotá to study at what she thought was "a classist, elitist university." "I was expecting to be bullied and that didn't happen, which made me very happy in my first semester," she remembers. Although most of her best friends were other scholarship students in her class, her extended circle of friends and acquaintances included several middle-class fellow students. Although she did not feel class was a barrier in her love relationship with her partner, she feared that his family was going to discriminate against her because of her social class. She had not met them yet, because her boyfriend's mother did not want him to be with her. The fact that the boyfriend was not from Bogotá helped them build a relationship that she believed would be more difficult otherwise.

In addition, some recognized condescendence as a class micro-aggression. Displays of explicit superiority, classism, or overt discrimination were not acceptable in a college environment marked by strong beliefs in meritocracy. Like in other contexts (Méndez & Gayo, 2018; Sherman, 2017), upper- and upper-middle-class students and their parents attempted to be inclusive and explicitly welcoming, but sometimes this seemed too artificial, condescending, or othering to lower-class students. For instance, when Laura, a psychology major, went to visit her upper-class boyfriend, his mother told her, "so you are *Pilo Paga*. You must be a genius!" in a tone that she described and mocked in the interview as condescending. She remembers feeling marked and very uncomfortable.

3.2.2 Gaps in Cultural Capital and Economic Conditions

Distances between lower- and upper-class students are not only geographic or in the means of transportation. They are manifested in everyday preferences, conversation topics, choice of where to eat lunch, how much to spend on it, or where to go out. These cultural and economic capital differences pose significant barriers to the formation of social capital, even when students share the same classroom and academic interests.

Stories of students who share that, upon arriving at the university, the topics of conversation about the travels and lifestyle of their privileged peers seemed disproportionate and very distant from their own realities, are recurrent. Jessica, for instance, describes some of the conversations she had at the beginning of her studies with her friends:

> I don't know, I felt out of place because they obviously talked about other sorts of things, that like, well, I'm not, it's not that usual for me . . . Like going out clubbing, or going on certain trips, I don't know. I remember at first, they spoke like of their trips to Europe, and I was fascinated, I was like, "that's so cool!" And it wasn't like it bothered them [that I couldn't join in the conversation], but like, yeah, I was lost and out of place [laughs]. Since all of them talked about something they had in common and I had nothing in common with them, It didn't feel nice. It wasn't like they treated me badly or made me feel bad, but [laughs] I don't know, I didn't feel comfortable.

Economic barriers to cross-class relations found their main expression around lunch. While most lower-class students brought lunch from home every day, most upper-class students went out for lunch every day. Notions of high and low prices differed significantly, even when those in the upper class tried to moderate their consumption. The same happened when going out. The places in the city where the upper-class students preferred to go were not only expensive but also situated far away from the homes of the lower-class students. Returning home after such outings was challenging, as public transportation was unavailable at night, and taxis or Ubers were expensive. Additionally, these transportation options sometimes avoided what drivers considered dangerous neighborhoods, where some SPP recipients lived.

3.2.3 Why Cross the Class Lines? The Benefits

These factors discouraging cross-class friendships resemble what many others have found in other contexts. However, in our case, the interesting aspect is that cross-class friendships did develop despite these challenges. Unlike in the US and other contexts where students often share dorms, our students lived in completely different neighborhoods and areas of the city, significantly reducing opportunities for interaction. Why did low-income students go to the effort of overcoming the costs associated with cross-class friendships? Why didn't they rely solely on the safety of homophilic relationships? We found that cross class friendships made lower-class students feel equally treated and, therefore, dignified. Feelings of relational equality in such an elite environment improved their sense of well-being and belonging. This relational equality emerged from daily interactions as equals but also by closer connections and intimacy with middle-class students. These friendships made them feel less like "strangers in paradise" (Reay, Crozier, & Clayton, 2009).

Most low-income students told us that after the harsh first days (for some, semesters) fearing discrimination, their well-being improved when they felt welcomed, equally treated, and recognized by other students, particularly, by their more upper-class friends. When Yeison, a very class-conscious political science student, went to his first party at a classmate's, he could not believe the luxury.

> With a friend we have a category and a name for everything. This was a party full of "aristohippies," from the French and the Italian schools [very elite schools], very thin, and very *gomelos* (local word for preppy). They speak very *gomelo*, but they dress all raggedy. They listen to pop, they listen to indie, they feel more comfortable with you but they don't stop being *gomelos*. They all live from 63rd street northards [the area of most concentrated affluence in the city]. So, we went to this party (...) And I felt shocked for a moment. A girl I really liked physically invited me. It was at her house. But she spoke and you could hear the *gomelo* accent really strong (...). She

> invited the whole class the second week of classes. I brought some cheap wine and some chicha [fermented corn popular beverage] with me, but they were all drinking like whiskey and I don't know what, and I was like oh, what happened here? Her dad came and gave us some rum and it was a Cuban rum, a very expensive thing. I had never tried it. I was happy drinking my chicha and my cheap wine. At that moment, I sensed a difference, like something was unusual. I was on the balcony (...) and this guy, who is now a close friend, showed up. He is an "aristohippie." "Want a cigarette?" he asked, and that led us downstairs to smoke together.

While the university served as a common and somehow equalizing space, visiting upper-class friends' houses prompted scholarship students to confront the stark economic and lifestyle inequalities between them and their classmates. At the same time, some of those encounters made them feel relationally equal, empowering them and fostering a sense of belonging. They also discovered that many classmates were more similar to them than they initially thought; they came from upwardly mobile families, their parents were in debt to pay for their education, or they had faced various economic difficulties as well. Being in the same classroom, engaging in conversations, and socializing helped diminish initial prejudices and fears of discrimination, aligning with Allport's (1954) predictions. As one scholarship student put it, "the veil fell, and we saw the humans."

A very important equalizing force in these relationships was the merit-based nature of the scholarships, instilling a sense of empowerment and deservingness among scholarship students. Sara illustrates this feeling of worthiness, equality, and dignity when she expressed:

> I think it's ridiculous to hide that you are on a scholarship. Yes, I have a scholarship! So what?! It is thanks to my knowledge, to the fact that I made an effort, to my skills, that I am here.

Moreover, it made them feel as magnets in relationships because sometimes others asked them for help. An upper-class graduate history student told us that "academically, the *pilos* added a lot to the classes. Because they studied a lot, they read everything, they were very good. And you felt you had to follow that level." However, academic excellence was a double-edged sword in a context of such enormous educational gaps. Despite having very good scores in the state exams, many scholarship students realized some classmates had had a much better education in their elite bilingual high schools.

Another benefit of having inter-class connections that many lower-class students often mentioned and appreciated was learning valued cultural capital from their more upper-class fellow students, from different experiences to new types of food. Middle-class friends or "privileged poor" (Jack, 2019) friends were crucial in bridging cultural capital. Some became "cultural guides"

(Lareau, 2015) to many lower-class students, teaching them about cuisines, manners, or places, albeit sometimes exercising different forms of symbolic violence. For example, Daniela told Ana Sofía not to use the dress she had bought for graduation because she considered it not to be appropriate for those events. Coming from a similar background but having gone to a middle-class private high school with a scholarship, she was trying to help her friend to fit in in at the party. Class aesthetics was the elephant in the room of this conversation, and it unveils, as mentioned earlier, an extra harsh demand on women to act and appear middle class:

> She told me that she needed to help me choose the dress because there were aspects to consider. For example, the dress shouldn't be very short or have a low neckline, and red was more for evening dresses than it was day dresses. She told me that something casual like trousers and a blazer or skirt and a blazer was better for a graduation, something formal and that didn't look like a *quinceañera*[6] dress. Clearly, I had already bought my dress, so I did the opposite of what she told me [laughs].
>
> **-So, you wore the one you bought?**
>
> -I ignored her (. . .). I was happy with my dress hahahahaha (. . .) It was my first time I wore a dress of my own. The only other time I had worn a dress was when I turned 15 and that dress was borrowed from a neighbor. Now that I had the opportunity, I bought one that *I* wanted (. . .). I don't regret it hahahaha. Although of course, I did feel a little uncomfortable at the ceremony, but oh well . . .

Only very rarely did we find explicit mentions of an instrumental or strategic search for contacts by lower-class students. Yet, Daniel, from one of the opening vignettes in Section 1, is an interesting case in point:

> - I always try not to let them notice that I am a scholarship student (a *becado*). (. . .)
>
> **- And why is that? Why do you try not to let them notice?**
>
> - Because I think I'm not going to have the same contacts, so to speak. Let's say I need a favor in the future; if they think you're like them, then it's easier, but if you say "I'm poor, I come from a certain neighborhood," there may be some stigma attached to that and they might think "it's better not to trust this person; they don't have the same education as we do." So, I try not to let them realize that I have a scholarship.

So, how did students like Daniel and others managed to build and maintain relationships with classmates who belong to other social worlds? Daniel

[6] In Colombia, like in many other places in Latin America, a girl's 15th birthday marks an important milestone and families generally put on a big celebration, including a flamboyant dress for the girl herself.

illustrates one of the most common mechanisms we found, camouflage. In the following section, we detail three types of strategies that scholarship students developed to deal with cross class connections and overcoming the relational costs: camouflaging, disclosure, and omnivorousness.

3.3 Class Relational Work in Cross-class Relations

3.3.1 Camouflaging

The main strategy that many low socioeconomic status students took to engage in cross-class relationships was to try to camouflage with their more upper-class friends. To do so, they needed to learn and emulate, and sometimes hide or carefully manage information about their background in a playing field that is by no means levelled, in which some manners, preferences, and lifestyles are more valued than others. Extreme and rare cases imply "faking it" as in Granfield's (1991) study, never admitting to being scholarship students, or omitting exactly where they live. As one student told us, "I tell them I live in the South but not exactly where." In most cases, however, it implied just blending in without foregrounding where they come from. "If they ask me, I tell them," was a recurrent phrase. Camouflaging requires quickly learning many implicit and often confusing cultural capital markers, such as ways of speaking or dress codes. Yet, with colleges like this one becoming increasingly more class diverse, as one elite student explained, it is still easy to spot the extremely elite students, but not the rest. In his words, "here, it is easy to know who is a *gomelo* but you cannot tell who has a scholarship from who doesn't." Hence, social mixing eases camouflaging.

Camouflaging has different limitations given the already mentioned high barriers for cross-class friendships. One clear such barrier is money. If the low socioeconomic status student does not want to expose herself, and the upper-class friend does not realize or does not adapt her consumption behavior, the consequence might be distancing. This was the case for Alejandra and two of her friends who had lunch at a gourmet burger chain everyday. Alejandra could not keep up with that level of spending and resorted to making excuses such as "I can't today, I need to leave early." In time, they stopped inviting her.

3.3.2 Disclosure

In some instances, instead of camouflaging and adapting to their more upper-class friends, low socioeconomic status students dared to expose their class of origin and negotiate with friends about the barriers in their relationships. Disclosure can be costly, especially when it leads to conflict. Laura, for example, gained confidence after a first semester of trying to camouflage, and finally dared to voice that she could not afford the expensive lunches her friends spent their money on. In her words,

> To have lunch with a friend, I would end up spending more than what I could afford for the day. But I have always been critical, like "How are we going to pay $12,000 pesos for this?" I started to make enemies, in part because I was critical with everything, with all the prices around this university.

In some other instances, disclosure and its negotiations were facilitated by both parts, such as when those with more resources deliberately chose a reasonably priced place to go out, in order to include everyone.

Time gave *becados* the strength for disclosure. The already-mentioned examples of Ana Sofía and her graduation dress and Daniel's proud social media post of his graduation are good examples of this. While camouflaging was the most common strategy to initiate inter-class interactions at the beginning, often associated with fear or shame, disclosure became more common in time as scholarship students gained the confidence to speak openly to their classmates.

3.3.3 Omnivorousness

Most *becados* took pride in exploring new tastes, places, and experiences from their new more upper-class acquaintances and friends. They mixed camouflaging with disclosure depending on the context, the level of trust in their relationship, and their own confidence. In the process, they became more culturally and socially omnivorous than their more privileged classmates.

Brahian summarizes his journey very clearly. He defines himself as "a peasant who had the opportunity to pursue an education." He comes from a small rural town in Santander, a department in the north-central Colombia, where he moved back after completing his studies. Engaging in local politics, he describes his experience in distant Bogotá and the socially distant university environment emphasizing the social capital he gained. For some time he had a picture of him with the former Provost of the University in one of his social networks. He looked visibly proud. He remembers thinking that "he had hit his head" when he entered the university because,

> It was like being in a totally different world and I don't know, having the opportunity to speak with a senator, to see the President and exchange a few words, or simply go swimming in the pool . . . It is a privilege. It's sad that not all of us have this privilege and that's why it's a responsibility at the same time. That is what has driven me to become involved in politics, to help others.

Living in two worlds was not easy. As he explained:

- You have to reconcile, reconcile. I've spent my life (...) navigating between different worlds, but it's very cool because tomorrow I can be at [the University alumni club] with friends having wine and the next day I can be speaking with peasants somewhere rural.

- **I say you become cultural omnivores.**

- [Laughing and approving] You have to work on it a lot. I kept telling myself: I study at [Study University], but I am not going to change. The way people treat each other at [Study University] is very horizontal, so that helps (...). But like my sister says, you have to "be clear about who you are, where you come from and where you are going." These are things that you have to check on all the time.

Over time, some lower-class students become culturally and socially omnivorous, chamaleonically (Abrahams & Ingram, 2013) moving from one class environment to another, and engaging in code-switching as needed. This adaptive behavior aligns with findings from similar research conducted in England by Crozier et al. (2019). Managing two worlds, two types of friends, two environments, requires extra work; however, as it has for Brahian, this effort translates into significant life gains. The code switching omnivorousness these individuals exhibit serves as a strategic approach for social mobility. It also has the potential to mitigate the harsh emotional toll associated with a fragmented self or the complete assimilation and detachment from one's original community, as documented in literature on upwardly mobile individuals (Bourdieu, 2007; Friedman, 2016; Lehmann, 2014; Morton, 2019). While existing literature has explored the cultural omnivorousness of the affluent (Khan, 2011), the phenomenon of the poor, not only becoming culturally but also socially omnivorous is an area worth exploring further, recognizing the inherent contradictions (Friedman, 2012), but also its possibilities (Streib, 2017).

Interestingly, the three identified strategies of relational work for navigating cross-class environments and building diverse networks are individualistic in nature. Unlike some colleges in the United States, where first-generation students, particularly among Afro communities, may form a collective identity that serves as a supportive and protective space, those in Colombia lack a similar shared identity. These collective identities can offer not only protection but also valuable learning strategies and the pride associated with a positive group experience. The absence of such collective identities among first-generation students in Colombia highlights a distinct challenge in fostering a shared sense of belonging and support within this demographic (Aries, 2008; Jack, 2019; Lee & Harris, 2020).

3.4 Beyond Relational Costs: Catching Up Academically and with the Institutional Hidden Curriculum

In this section, I have attempted to contribute theoretically to understanding the challenges faced by underprivileged groups entering privileged environments, focusing specifically on the costs associated with engaging in heterogeneous relationships and the requisite relational work. However, it is important to acknowledge that relational costs are not the sole hurdles confronted by students from lower socioeconomic backgrounds. A substantial part of their effort was directed toward catching up academically, including learning the hidden curriculum. Studying at an elite university with a high academic level demanded a significant investment from these *becados*. Beyond dedicating more time and resources to enhance their skills, they also felt a constant pressure, responsibility, and anxiety stemming the uncertainty of whether or not they will be able to meet the academic requirements. As mentioned earlier, most scholarship students come from underfunded state schools. Many of them told us that, while they thought they were really good students based on their previous academic experiences, they felt insecure and underprepared when they entered the university.

The negative consequences of these academic disadvantages were less evident in their academic outcomes than in terms of their emotional distress (Corredor, González-Arango, & Corredor et. al. 2020b). In fact, the *pilos*' grades were, on average, similar to those of regular students, controlling for program, while dropout rates were lower.[7] Yet, maintaining these positive academic results while dealing with the stress of having to repay the condonable loan in the event of noncompletion exerted overwhelming pressure on the *pilos*. The cumulative pressures compounded for many who had to leave their hometowns to study in the capital, resulting in a lack of the familiar social support offered by family and community. Also, issues such as delayed subsidies led to them having insufficient funds for transportation or meals on certain days.

One of the biggest academic challenges for most *pilos* at Study University was their level of English proficiency. Despite the availability of English classes at the university, *pilos* felt overwhelmed due to the extensive amount of readings in English within regular classes, often all in the same semester. This demand not only presented an academic challenge but also served a class marker.

The assumption that university students are proficient in English as a second language is just one facet of the broader issue. Elite colleges often harbor additional layers of hidden curriculum that translate into cultural capital, thereby transforming into learning costs for scholarship students. During an informal conversation with two students, they reported an instance in which

[7] Author's analysis based on administrative data from the Study University for all 2020 graduates.

a professor at Study University mentioned a painting in a European museum as if everybody knew it. In response, these students resourcefully got together after class, to look it up on the internet and catch up, but they felt they were the only ones that did not understand the reference and they did not want the others to discover they had never heard of that painting.

There are many subtle ways in which institutions assume specific cultural capital from students. Elite institutions like the one in this study are accustomed to empowered students that ask questions, come to office hours, write emails to professors, and ask for flexibility if they cannot turn in an exam. As in Jack's (2016) study, scholarship students have to learn that "there's no harm in asking."

3.5 Institutional Variation

While academic costs were consistently high across different institutions, relational costs proved to be notably elevated in elite environments. Elsewhere, we draw comparisons with data from different institutional contexts (Corredor et al., 2020a). However, this books' fieldwork uncovered a rare natural experiment that serves as a valuable illustration of this phenomenon:

> Valeria, the exceptional student in the very problematic high school we met in the previous section, and Johanna had a common childhood. They lived together since they were nine years old, when Johanna's parents passed away and she moved with her grandmother, Valeria's mom, to a small town outside of Bogotá. Although one is a niece and the other is the aunt, they always say, "we are like sisters." They share their bedroom. They went to the same high school, which Johanna also defines as problematic because of gangs, drugs, and very bad teachers in some subjects. Yet, they were both among the good students in that school. The care, presence, and strict rules imposed by grandma-mom, who controlled their friends and their activities, and rare yet exceptional schoolteachers, like their biology teacher, were perhaps behind the success of both girls in their state exam. Their peer group, which they also shared, helped as well. "We were the hard working ones," Valeria said. They both won the SPP scholarship. Both wanted to study at the national public university. Yet only Johana got in. Her score in the specific university entrance exam was not high enough to study what she initially wanted, but it was enough for psychology. Valeria, on the other hand, after an enormous disappointment, decided to use her scholarship to go Study University, a more elite environment she feared. Their paths diverged at this point, creating a natural experiment to evaluate the impact of class mixing in college environments on social integration and, potentially, social mobility.
>
> Johana and Valeria both faced academic challenges and felt at a disadvantage in terms of cultural capital compared with their classmates, just as the literature has described for other contexts. In Johanna's own words,

> Many many classmates here have a very high cultural and symbolic capital, so they know a lot, the way they express themselves, what they say, what they know about politics, (. . .) You feel bad. It's like, I'm so dumb. I wish I weren't here. So, it was up to you to study. (. . .) But it is interesting because if you do things well, you come out well prepared.

However, these gaps did not stop her or put her at risk of dropping out. The environment was friendlier, and less elitist, in her public university, than what her aunt described. Her relational costs, that is, the costs of making friends and particularly of building diverse networks, were lower in an environment that she described as "harmonic" and "diverse" in terms of class and place of origin. "I feel comfortable," she said. Valeria, in contrast, felt like a "stranger in paradise" (Reay et al., 2009). Although she does not admit being discriminated against because of her class, she did find a hostile environment in which some classmates did not talk to her, and one individual went so far as to condescendingly remark, "Poor you!" when she shared information about where she lived (Bosa, a lower-class locality in Bogotá).

While Johanna adapted smoothly, feeling welcome, safe, and stimulated in her new environment in the public university, dominated by middle- and lower-class students, without great divides, Valeria had a terrible first experience in her more elitist college, even though she entered with many other scholarship students.[8] She felt lonely and overwhelmed, especially with the extensive English reading requirements, so she decided to suspend her first semester. Luckily, she came back and managed to graduate, but her experience was much less enjoyable than her niece's.

This rare quasi-natural experiment of two almost sisters in two different contexts reveals that institutional variation in terms of socioeconomic heterogeneity and institutional culture can determine how lower-class students adapt (Aries & Seider, 2005; Corredor et al., 2020a). Within the elite institution, we also found variation by program, depending on class heterogeneity, but also on professional cultures. For example, scholarship students felt much more welcomed in engineering or in the social sciences than in law, where they faced a more classist environment.

3.6 Conclusion

The case of scholarship students entering an elite university in Colombia provides a unique lens through which we can observe unlikely cross-class interactions and,

[8] Most incoming students in Universidad Nacional de Colombia in Bogotá belong to socioeconomic stratum 3 or lower. In 2016, the year in which Johana entered, half of the incoming students were stratum 2 or lower, that is, similar to her (Estadísticas UNAL). In contrast, when Valeria entered Study University, she found that only about 25 percent of the students were like her, and that was exceptional because of the scholarship program. She also found much more elite students, coming from elite schools that choose not to attend public universities.

therefore, the possibility of building diversified networks, which, in turn, may serve as a mechanism for social mobility. While much is known about segregation in educational and other environments, there is limited understanding of what transpires when individuals from disparate socioeconomic backgrounds converge, and the intricate dynamics within these relationships.

In doing so, this research makes a valuable contribution to the broader literature on the costs of college integration and upward mobility. Traditionally, this literature has focused on cultural capital gaps, conflicts, and associated costs. However, this study brings to light another significant cost: the effort involved in building social capital. Social capital is a crucial asset that can play a pivotal role in effectively achieving desired social mobility.

This case study teaches us about the possibilities of cross-class interactions and unveils the unevenly distributed costs and efforts associated with them, often borne by the less privileged individuals. In doing so, this research makes a valuable contribution to the broader literature on the costs of college integration and upward mobility, diverging from the predominant focus on cultural capital gaps, conflicts, and costs. Specifically, this research brings attention to an often-overlooked dimension: the cost of building social capital – a pivotal asset essential for effectively attaining desired social mobility. Unlike the prevailing literature on mixing in college, which tends to underscore issues such as isolation, homophily, and related costs, this research uniquely accentuates the presence and advantages of cross-class interactions. Notably, it emphasizes the positive impact on lower-class students, highlighting their symbolic belonging to the educational institution and their cultivation of middle-class cultural capital, which may serve them for social mobility in the future.

While same-class interactions were much easier, and a source of security and identification, students from low socioeconomic backgrounds actually did not confine themselves solely to segregated networks. Our study contributes to existing literature on similar elite contexts by highlighting the intricacies of cross-class relationships (Lee, 2016; Zelizer & Gaydosh, 2019). It does so for a particularly unequal context, not only in terms of the institution, but also in terms of the broader national and regional context, where youth trajectories are often completely segregated, and upward mobility opportunities exceptionally low. This extreme context is methodologically useful because it magnifies both the costs and the strategies to overcome them. It also underscores an important condition behind the possibility of fostering cross-class interactions, reminiscent of Allport's (1954) contact theory: the presence of conditions of equality (merit in this case) and extended contact time. However, mixing and contact do not happen automatically; they require relational work, and if institutions fail to change, the work rests mainly on the shoulders of those who have to adapt.

4 Getting Out

This section addresses the transitions to the labor market that graduates from lower-class background experience, marking the final phase in this longitudinal follow-up of the SPP program and many of its students. Transitions to the labor market are a pivotal moment in the realm of social mobility, serving as a juncture characterized by the potential for gate opening, opportunity hoarding, and social closure. The SPP program undoubtedly facilitates social mobility by providing high-quality higher education to most of its participants and their families. This fact cannot be overlooked or dismissed by the flattening power of reproduction theory. Their transition from college to the workforce and their first experiences in the labor market are, however, far from smooth. The challenges they encounter are largely contingent not on the students – who, as previously noted, exhibit comparable performance to their peers on average – but on the characteristics of the labor markets they navigate. Lower-quality and more elitist labor markets are more difficult for social mobility. The hurdles to entering are higher. In such environments, having a degree is not enough. The barriers imposed by the class ceiling are more pronounced (Friedman & Laurison, 2019).

The following interview extract featuring Daniel, the law student we already know, who has since graduated and is now a (indebted) graduate student abroad, illustrates many of the arguments outlined in this section.

- **Ok. And if you had to describe the process of looking for a job, how would you do it? How have you felt when looking for a job? Happy, excited, worried, hopeless? What comes to mind when you think about it?**
- Mmmmm, what can I say, well, in that area I feel kind of discouraged. Yes, like, what's the point of studying at Study University? If this is the best university, then you are supposed to be able to get certain jobs. (. . .)

- **Your perception of the labor market is that it is difficult, let's say.**
- Yes, and that if it is not with the right person, the recommendation, no matter what merits you have, you are not going to get in. At least in state jobs, right? On the government side. Maybe in the private sector it is a little different. Although it is also works by recommendation, but maybe it is a little bit different, and maybe it is not about personal connections as much as it is in the public sector.

- **And why is it that this private sector does not draw your attention so much? Some lawyers we have interviewed have told us about firms. It is a very particular sector and lawyers have different opinions about them. What is yours?**

- Well, I feel that the law firm environment is the environment I lived in during my first semesters of law school and I didn't like it. Not at all. I am not going to go there to be humiliated. Maybe I would earn more money because they do earn well. And if they humiliate themselves, if they humiliate themselves in the right way, they emerge. And hat's not for me.

- **Can you tell me a little bit more about that environment? Could you describe it?**
- Well, it's always like, how should I put it. If you're so-and-so's friend, if you came out of such-and-such school, then they tend to view you more favorably. If you are prettier, you are more likely to stand out. It's an environment of humiliation. Many law school classmates are aware that it's a longstanding tradition, and they graduate knowing that the initial months in firms can be quite demeaning. You have to carry the files, run from here to there, from one building to another, carrying papers, carrying the coffees, but then you are already a junior partner. And I don't want to do that. How come? And besides, I don't like private law.

- **Ok, so frankly, it is a sector that you have not thought of applying to, nor are you interested in it.**
- I'm not interested.

- **Would you describe the firms' environment as classist?**
- Yes, yes, yes, yes.

- **Okay. Could you elaborate a little bit more? In what sense?**
- Well, it's the same as in college. For example, I didn't have much of a relationship with the men because they were like that. If you didn't talk about a certain subject, if you didn't dress a certain way, if you weren't in their circle, you were nobody. I didn't like that environment at all. (. . .) When I took classes in Government, it wasn't like that. You could talk about politics, society, law, and it was not such a tense and stupid atmosphere. I could never connect with the men in Law. (Laughs) On the other hand, women were a little more open, no? Also, because I was a gay friend, but there was a healthier way of relating to each other, I would say.

This interview excerpt starts with a sense of unmet expectations and disappointment. Many of the scholarship students followed their heart in deciding what to study, giving little thought to the labor market. They lacked vocational guidance or career planning. Entering an elite private institution led them to believe that success in the labor market was almost guaranteed. On average, they were right.

Indeed, according to a quantitative impact evaluation study examining the medium-term effects of SPP in the labor market, the program contributes to narrowing the gap between rich and poor graduates in enrollment, graduation, learning, and entrance salaries (Londoño-Vélez et al., 2022). Compared to similar low-income high achievers who just missed the eligibility threshold for the program, scholarship students exhibit superior outcomes in terms of access to education, quality of institutions, graduation rates, entry into formal jobs, and salary levels.

However, the dynamics of the labor market vary across specific careers, with cultural and social capital weighing differently in different professions and areas, making them more or less elitist and closed for newcomers. Thus, when Daniel emphasizes that merit alone is not enough, and that connections matter, he echoes the sentiments expressed by many lower-class graduates from Law and other equally elitist or lower-quality labor markets. Like many other scholarship students, he has found it impossible to get a labor contract, often working in short-term positions, involving legal advice and research. Despite his aspirations to work in the public sector, he has found it difficult to break into that realm. Additionally, like many other lower-class law graduates, he expresses strong reservations about working in law firms, perceiving them as classist environments that demand specific cultural capital, particularly proficiency in English and adherence to particular norms of speech and dress. In contrast, lower-class graduates from fields in which social and cultural capital are not that relevant at entry level faced fewer barriers.

As we will later see, regardless of their achievements in the labor market, many scholarship students, including Daniel, seek additional sources of income. He has invested and worked in his family business, as a safety net in case of unforeseen circumstances. This sense of vulnerability and concern for the future is something we found across scholarship graduates and not in their upper-class peers. This concern is sometimes exacerbated by the precarious nature of the labor contracts available in a highly flexible and informal labor market.

4.1 The Winners

Álvaro is a biomedical engineering graduate, self-trained as a big data and artificial intelligence engineer, currently working at a quantum computing US-based startup company. He left a position as data engineer at an international bank once he felt he had reached a learning ceiling there. His salary is higher than all the other interviewees, regardless of their socioeconomic background (it is actually even higher than mine). He entered a thriving labor market in a niche industry. And for the first time in his life, his mind was at ease in terms of his finances. He lives on his own and helps his grandmother, who raised him. I met Álvaro in one of his elective classes, and I followed him for several years. We became close and I witnessed how he came up against several barriers throughout college. He dropped out of high school out of necessity, and was working when he decided to take the state exam, in which he excelled. Serendipitously, in that same year, his performance made him beneficiary of an SPP scholarship. He had never dreamed of studying at a private university. It was not easy. He had to move to Bogotá. He was older than his classmates. It was difficult to make friends. He was in risk of dropping out at least twice for financial and personal reasons. The pandemic hit when he was in his final semesters. He faced challenges with limited internet access for studying in his room in a boarding house. But, he persevered, even resorting to crowdfunding at one point, and ultimately graduated. His resourcefulness knew no bounds and despite him realizing relatively early that he would have liked computer/industrial engineering or physics better, he could not go back. Paying a semester on his own was unthinkable. Savvy and autodidact, he started to build his CV in preparation for the labor market. He started to take Coursera courses and contacting people in the field. Unable to help with computer engineering, I helped him build his LinkedIn profile in English. This turned out to be a very successful strategy, and together with contacts through other professors, both in Colombia and abroad, he was very successful in building his social capital. The last time I saw him, he treated me to lunch. "I want to invite you like you invited me so many times."

Like Álvaro, all the computer engineers that we interviewed were working in their fields after, and some even before, graduation. Their transition proved to be relatively smooth, and, overall, the labor market felt less stressful than studying. Even those without the best grades were working. Their experience in the labor market was not that different from the experience of individuals belonging to the upper class. This, of course, does not imply a complete absence of gaps or difficulties in the process but, rather, a comparative reduction in such challenges.

The law graduates that we interviewed were all working as well and were in a clear process of upward mobility when compared to their parents. They had studied more or in a more prestigious institution, they were earning more, they were accessing better jobs and consumption goods that their parents would have never dreamt of at their age or even today. They were also much better off than their best friends from high school. However, in contrast to the computer engineers, they had felt the weight of their lack of the adequate cultural and social capital to enter some of the most prestigious jobs among young lawyers: private firms. Their experience is very different from their upper-class peers, whose cultural and social capital derived from their upbringing and high school – rather than higher education – played a pivotal role in entering the labor market without any of those barriers. Factors such as bilingualism with a flawless native English accent, appropriate attire, and other forms of cultural alignment, along with influential contacts, made their transitions smoother. Rodrigo, for example, hailing from an affluent background, and having attended a private bilingual school before college, effortlessly joined one of his father's – a prestigious criminal lawyer – firms. Similarly, Sebastián leveraged connections from his elite bilingual high school to secure a recommendation and contact to enter the firm in which he has been for the last three years.

All but one of the scholarship lawyers we interviewed had avoided entering private firms. His experience, although unique, sheds light on how difficult it is to enter and assimilate into those firms, and why some prefer to steer clear of such environments. Duvan was able to enter a firm despite not meeting the English language requirements, thanks to a recommendation from a former TA who was already working there and who recognized his talent. He describes the working environment as harsh, or classist, akin to Daniel's perspective. He shared an incident where a colleague, apparently wanting to serve as a cultural guide (Lareau, 2015), told him not to wear a suit from a certain middle-priced Colombian store (Arturo Calle), cautioning that he might appear like a doorman.

Duvan does not include his status as an SPP fellow in his CV, as others do, because "firms are very elitist." He adopts a strategic camouflage, becoming a cultural omnivore to navigate the professional landscape. "I have already learned a lot about restaurants. I have been to Osaki" (an Asian restaurant), he proudly stated. Meanwhile, he is paying for his younger sister to take English classes to spare her from the challenges he faced and urges his parents to enroll her in a private school.

In contrast, all other lower-class lawyers we interviewed either were already working in or aspired to work in the public sector or in labor law. Some came to this conclusion after realizing that the world of prestigious firms, highly coveted at their university, was not fit for them because they did not have the contacts. Others were sure that they wanted to pursue different avenues within the legal profession from the outset.

4.2 Fear of Falling: The Emotions of Social Mobility Resurface

The transition to the labor market marks a moment in which emotions associated to social class and mobility (Friedman, 2014, 2016; Reay, 2005) once again come to the forefront for graduates from lower-class backgrounds, echoing the emotional landscape experienced when initially entering college. The emotional ambivalence inherent in social mobility resurfaces during this pivotal transition to adulthood. Even those from lower-class background that we might consider successful grapple with stress, fear, anguish, and a sense of urgency, uncertainty, and insecurity. Their experiences are reminiscent of the anxieties depicted in Ehrenreich's (2020) exploration of the professional middle class in the United States. However, in Colombia, a history of precarity and substantial family responsibilities adds an extra burden for lower-class graduates who urgently need to find a stable salary. These negative emotions are particularly pronounced among those like Daniel, who face difficulties in finding employment, leading to a sense of disappointment. In contrast, their upper-class counterparts often lean more toward confidence and tranquility. Moreover, certain working environments evoke feelings of displacement reminiscent of their initial experiences when entering college. These negative emotions coexist with happiness, fulfillment, and personal, family and even community pride stemming from the accomplishment of completing a degree, securing decent jobs, and finally achieving their goals.

Jefferson remembered his last semesters at the university as tinged with anguish. In contrast to his more privileged upper-class peers, he refrained from taking on practicums or part-time jobs during his college years. He felt he had to concentrate on his studies to excel and avoid any risk of losing his scholarship. Thus, despite being one of the best students of his generation, he felt very insecure and anguished as he approached graduation. He remembered thinking:

> "What am I going to do for work?" I started to pass resumés and nah, they asked for English everywhere, my karma, the cross I bear, has been not having studied English. They ask for English everywhere. I applied to BBVA bank by mistake because they didn't specify that you needed to have English in order to be considered. "Oh, the first job where you don't need to know English, let's go for it," I thought. I went through all the filters and when I got to the penultimate filter, they asked, "well, how is your English." And I said: "no, I am applying for this job because they didn't ask for English" (laughs). (. . .) [They said] no, we are sorry, what a mess, (. . .) They rejected me for not knowing any English, so I was very pissed. But I thought, "well, in the end I need to make money, so if I have to go out to do something other than law, then I will do something else." The world of work was very uncertain for me.

He was considering leaving the field of law when a former TA contacted him to work with another professor at the university. Recognizing his exceptional abilities, this professor, in turn, encouraged him to pursue a career as a law clerk with aspirations of becoming a judge one day. The professor went on to recommend Jefferson, who subsequently took a test and passed an interview, and was selected for the position. He was extremely happy with his new job, for how stimulating it was and because a very good salary allowed him to take care of his extended family (mom, sister, partner, and baby). With his monthly earning of US$1,500, he now feels like a "multimillionaire."

> So I love my job, I love it, I think it is cool, I can see myself doing it for a long time. But, I am tired, I need to rest, I need a break, I need to get away from everything. I am very privileged, seriously, who gets a job where they pay, they pay me very well. Right now I am a multimillionaire; literally, I have given myself luxuries that my family would never have been able to afford, going out to lunch at a good restaurant at least two Sundays a month, incredible, restaurants, it's crazy, incredible menus, delicious things to eat. I am assuming all the expenses of my household, all of them, the house payments, I even bought a truck, so (laughs) those payments for that truck, the food, everything and I am doing very well, I am not overpaid, I am relaxed, and I have even set aside some savings. The salary is fantastic, and the workload is reasonable. In State jobs, they don't exploit you, I think, what I have seen, they don't exploit me in labor terms, sometimes they have very high standards, though.

We see the emotional ambivalence in Jefferson's words. Pride and fulfillment intertwine with feelings of being overwhelmed by responsibilities. In his work environment, Jefferson feels valued, respected, and challenged. Yet, informal interactions are sometimes uncomfortable in an upper-class environment. In his own words:

> - I feel like a fish out of water when there are these integration activities, coincidentally this Friday there is a bowling outing because the boss is celebrating 4 years in his position. (...) If it were solely up to me, I wouldn't go, I would rather spend time with my son and my wife. These kinds of gatherings bore me. I don't know, we are from different contexts, you know what I mean?
>
> - **Tell me about these kinds of gatherings and why you are from different contexts.**
> - Well, because they are going to talk about what master's degree someone will do at Harvard, about who finished such and such at Yale. They sometimes give out very cool academic tips, like, books they recommend and things like that, what book summarize important information and everything, so I try to be receptive to that. But when they start talking about "oh, I went to the United States to get vaccinated and I took the opportunity to do such and such," well, I can't contribute much to the conversation because I haven't been to the United States. So, it's those kinds of discussions where I don't have much to add.
>
> I'm going to do a master's degree at Harvard too but it's not an immediate need or possibility for me [he is currently finishing two MAs, locally] For example, I would like to talk more about the state of the country, literally, the elections. However, it's not feasible with some of my colleagues because it's considered politically incorrect, and we do not know who might be related to those individuals with certain last names. These aspects limit my discussions (...). I feel much more at ease with the office secretary, the driver, and the judges. In those circles, I sense more freedom, fewer masks in the

> conversations, and a more transparent and relaxed atmosphere. It's interesting; when the judges get drunk (laughs), when they get drunk they become uninhibited and start to relax and talk about things without always wanting to be politically correct.

Jefferson's experience and emotional ambivalences contrast highly with those of Federico, an upper-class law graduate who described these three years after graduation as "the best in my life." He contrasts his experience after graduation with the academic challenges he faced at university. Studying was hard. Law is very hierarchical. He took an extra year to finish slowly. He wanted to think. He had doubts about becoming a lawyer. In contrast, finding a job felt easier. He rejected a job offer from his dad. He did not want help. Upon returning from a graduation trip vacation, he swiftly found a job. While he received offers from law firms, he was hesitant about the prospect of being "exploited" there. Instead, he decided to apply for a job he found through the university employment service. He entered an international company that provides subscribed users legal information and is now working as a business manager there. In contrast to Jefferson, Federico feels at complete ease with his co-workers. In his words,

> [they are, in general], incredible people with an incredible culture and yes, personally, I can tell you that I have gotten very drunk with my bosses in their houses, in mine. We have a very good personal relationship, but always respectful at work. So, I have no doubt that these last three years have been the best of my life.

Federico's story introduces a nuanced perspective to Khan's (2011) definition of privilege. While privilege can indeed be manifested in carrying oneself with ease, it also encompasses the freedom to doubt, fail, transition to adulthood without feeling fear of falling or losing it all.

4.3 "You Never Know What Might Happen": Economic Insecurity and *Rebusque*

While emotional ambivalences associated to mobility are difficult to cope with, they drive lower-class students to be resourceful and to seek additional sources of income (from investments to side jobs). This, resourcefulness is an asset they bring to the labor market and that some employers recognize. The feelings of uncertainty are even more present among those who have not found a good job yet. In the interviewees' words, "you can go to bed and not have a job the next day," "you have to have many different plans," or perhaps more clearly, "you have to try and get ahead in life" ("A uno le toca rebuscarse mucho en la vida").

Rebusque, in Spanish, is a very interesting and almost untranslatable term, used to illustrate the various ways most lower-class individuals make ends meet. They engage in diverse jobs, from cleaning and selling one day, to pursuing various side gigs. It is interesting to see these graduates inheriting this resourceful mindset from their families and implementing it in their adult lives. For example, we found a graduate investing in Bitcoin. Jefferson, while working as a judge, invested in a barber shop with an old friend from high school who was never able to continue studying. Daniel, as we saw, invests in his family business. This emerged as an unexpected finding during fieldwork and it consistently surfaced in interview after interview. The ability of lower-class background students to actively search for additional investments and sources of income, even if driven by a fear of falling or losing it all, adds a layer of resilience. While this coping mechanism may heighten psychological pressures and lead to burnout, it is crucial to underscore the advantages they bring to the labor market. As Streib (2017) has pointed out, we know more about social immobility than about social mobility and we know much less about the characteristics of the upwardly mobile. Recognizing and acknowledging this resourcefulness could position it as a valuable asset for firms seeking to identify unique strengths during job interviews.

4.4 Family Responsibilities

Ana Sofía, from the opening vignette, is one of the best students of her generation. She finished her BA in political science and an MA in sociology in record time. Her MA thesis earned an undisputed top grade of 5 (A+). Her employers praise her abilities as a highly qualified analyst and writer, with organizational skills and unmatchable ethical standards. She has worked as a researcher for two professors in short-term positions, but now holds a relatively stable job as a researcher with one of them. Because she graduated during the pandemic, working from home became a standard, which is comfortable for her because she lives in Bosa, a working-class locality in Bogotá with lots of transportation problems, so she saves money and time working from home. Besides, she can use the time she saves for side projects.

As mentioned earlier, she needs the money as she is the main provider for her household. Her boyfriend improvised a home office for her, as there was no room for one. She rents the first floor of a house for her mother, grandmother, a sister with a disability, and a teenage brother. Her mother is an informal domestic worker and hairdresser but is currently (at the time of our last interview) unable to work because of some surgery she had had. Although professors, including myself, told her she could go on to do a PhD wherever she wants, she has to stay for now. Once she buys a house for them, big enough so they can rent one of the rooms or set up a salon for her mom to work from home, she will be freer to leave if she still wants to.

Ana Sofía's story is one of social mobility in terms of education. Yet her narrative highlights the role of family responsibilities as a burden for many upwardly mobile youngsters, especially for women, who besides economic responsibilities tend to have more direct care responsibilities. For the most part, our upwardly mobile youngsters become the main providers of their households at a young age, paying for their siblings' education, their grandma's house repairs, or their mothers' healthcare needs. Symbolically, they gain status in their families, who are proud of their achievements. These family responsibilities may, however, slow down or hinder their individual mobility. The urgency to produce becomes substantial once they graduate, and they sometimes have to forgo interesting, yet precarious, jobs opportunities or opportunities to study abroad that their more privileged friends can seize more easily. On the positive side, these individuals do not experience the same sense of dislocation from their community, a phenomenon described in studies of upward mobility in the North (Bourdieu, 2007; Friedman, 2016).

4.5 The Disappointed

Like Daniel, we found other disappointed scholarship graduates facing lower-quality and more elitist labor markets. What we found to be behind this disappointment is the distance between expectations from a private elite university and the reality after graduation. Based on the longitudinal data, we were able to observe how some lower-class background students were compelled to adjust their expectations. One of them was Sara, the supermotivated business administration major who had increased her expectations and wanted to be a "successful businesswoman," in her second year of college.

When we interviewed Sara for the second time, her aspirations had changed considerably. Her dreams of being an entrepreneur had dwindled, during the pandemic, to simply finding a stable job. She graduated and left for the United States to improve her English while working as an au pair. She came back in the middle of the pandemic and found it extremely difficult to find a job. She describes those times as times of

> total uncertainty, I don't know, I can't tell you if it would have been different in a different context, but for me, the fact of being in this process right during the pandemic, I feel that it made everything a little bit more difficult (. . .) [I felt] a lot of uncertainty, then a little bit of anxiety, then a little bit of stress, then a little bit of panic, and more panic of no, nothing came up. If I am really honest

with you, to think about looking for another job today, as I am already tired here, I need to look for a job, it gives me a lot of mental stress, because it doesn't seem like a good process. (...) It was so difficult, the fact that companies never told me why they didn't want to hire me, you know? What did I do wrong?

Although the pandemic might have made the process more difficult, especially for some labor markets, none of the upper-class students mentioned these types of extreme difficulties. Sara's lack of social and economic capital did not help her find a job in what she wanted as an entrepreneur. Upon her return from the States, and following several unsuccessful jobs, a strong family tie proved to be instrumental.

- One of my mother's cousin is friends with someone who works at the National Federation of Coffee Growers (...) She had called me and asked me whether I had not been able to get a job, and I said I hadn't, this is difficult, bla, bla, bla, and she told me wait and see if I can talk to *Sultanita* to see if we know of any vacancies in the federation, and I was ready. Then she gave me the woman's contact, I passed her my resumé and the woman told me what she could do was to circulate my CV and "then you do the normal process" and I said "thank you very much." (...) So, they told me about a job vacancy, they told me what it was, obviously it fitted with what I wanted, with what I consider I am good at, the salary was better, yes, everything looked much better, so I applied, I had the interviews, and I passed.

- **Super, and what position is that at the federation?**
- It is called organizational development analyst (...) I have grown a lot, I do something that I really like (...) The Federation is a very good employer, I have really felt very satisfied with everything I have experienced, let's say in this long year, I have a fixed contract until the next month [laughs] and next month they change it to an indefinite one.

As the main provider at home together with her father, Sara needs a stable income. Her family ties were crucial in getting this job, but her story is very different from stories of upper-class graduates in business administration who can become entrepreneurs on their own or work within their family businesses. As Daniel put it, sometimes merit is not enough. And Sara's story is not the most extreme. Although she dreads the prospect of another job search, she managed to secure a stable and challenging position. Many in even lower-quality job markets, like in the social sciences, were still trying to find work. In these fields, lower salaries and short-term contracts increased feelings of disappointment.

Merit and effort are not always related to the positive outcomes students dreamt of when they entered an elite college. This varies a lot by career choice. Entering a harsh labor market, with lower salaries and less opportunities in general, where social and cultural capital carries more weight for securing better prospects, has been extremely difficult. In the process, the dreamers became quite disappointed.

4.6 Social Capital

In this final subsection, I want to go back to one of the inspirational questions of this research, that is, to what extent can social networks help the underprivileged attain social mobility.

Our interviews show that networks are indeed crucial in finding jobs. They are both crucial for the upper classes, who often rely on homogeneous social capital acquired before college, accumulated in the family, or in elite high schools where they form most of their lifetime friendships, and crucial for first-generation students who acquire useful social capital in college, especially those facing more elitist or lower-quality labor markets in which networks can make the difference. For example, Diana, an economics major, who formed more upper-class friendships during college, found her current job at a public opinion and consultancy firm because an upper-class friend, who already worked there and had contacts within the company, recommended her and helped her prepare for the selection process. In other cases, very weak ties were also useful. In the case of Andrés, another economics major, it was a much weaker, also upper-class, tie who helped him once. He was at a job interview for a startup, and he recognized the interviewer and owner of the startup. The interviewer remembered that they had taken classes together, and Andrés thinks that this made him choose him over other candidates.

Yet, as evident in most of the stories earlier, the most directly useful heterogeneous ties were not classmates, but professors and teaching assistants. These heterogeneous ties combine two features: more resources and close knowledge of the abilities and needs of their students. Had it not been for his TA and his professor, Jefferson would have quit law, in a critical juncture of needing to find a job to provide for his family.

This willingness to help from well-resourced cross-class ties (professors) is crucial factor that is often under-analyzed in the literature. Existing research tends to place significant trust in the mere circulation of opportunities and information. In contrast, social capital literature places more emphasis on weak cross-class ties to transfer nonredundant information and resources including job opportunities (Granovetter, 1977). Contrary to the prevailing notion, we observe that a certain level of closeness and direct intervention significantly facilitates the gate opening needed for social mobility. Close ties within the same class possess a dual strength: being part of a heterogeneous environment, they have access to opportunities and information they can pass on to friends. Simultaneously, due to the proximity of these relationships, they are more intimately aware of the challenges their friends face, and of how to help them. Thus, in many cases, it was other scholarship students who helped their friends find jobs either by recommending them, or passing on job offers, or by helping them with their CVs and interview preparation while they gave specific advice and emotional counseling from the perspective of a peer who went through similar experiences.

If direct weak and close ties are important for gate opening, exposure too is an important mechanism. Being in an environment with higher expectations elevates the expectations for everyone involved. However, as we observed, this dynamic can sometimes generate frustrations, as exemplified in the case of Sara. The willingness to purse MA programs in prestigious universities abroad is an example of these higher aspirations among scholarship students, as inspired by their more upper-class peers and their professors. Interestingly, however, such inspiration also derives from their same-class ties. Many mentioned hardworking successful scholarship students as their mentors or role models. For example, Luisa got her inspiration to study programming on her own from another scholarship student, and this led her to a much better job opportunity. Jefferson, in turn, mentioned being very moved by his friend's, a fellow *pilo*, professional accomplishments, especially the fact that he was building a house for his family in his hometown.

Table 3 summarizes these findings.

Table 3 Resources circulating through different ties and mechanisms in heterogeneous environments that foster social mobility.

	Same class	**Cross-class**
Weak ties	Information	Information Hiring
Strong ties	Information Opportunities Emotional support Specific instrumental support (e.g., help with CV)	Information Better opportunities Hiring Recommendations Specific instrumental support
Exposure	Peer effects (strategies to survive an elitist environment and feel supported) Role models among peers: ("if he could make it, I can make it too")	Peer effects in higher expectations (e.g., study an MA in Harvard or being an entrepreneur are possible) Role models (professors)

4.7 Conclusion

In contrast to its role in facilitating access the university, the SPP program did not directly help students in the labor market. In this regard, the program focused more on fostering equality of opportunity rather than ensuring equality of outcomes. By trusting the intelligence and resilience of these students, it opened a closed door and let them in. This shows, without doubt, the power of opportunity. A majority of these students have successfully completed their education, and many of them are currently undergoing various processes of upward mobility in relation to their past and their parents. However, the labor market door is not equally opened to all. While a degree from a prestigious institution holds significant importance, its weight depends on the labor market. Additionally, in different professions, the significance of social and cultural capital in securing employment differs. First-generation students face more challenges in low-quality and elitist labor markets, where cultural and social capital play a more significant role.

Regarding social capital, a diversified network that combines heterogeneous and homogeneous, and weak and close, ties seems to be the most helpful for those in need of them to enter these types of more difficult job markets.

5 Final Thoughts

This Element tells an unlikely story, one of mostly successful upwardly mobile youth in an unequal and segregated context. It acknowledges the power of public policy and education to open crucial opportunities that were previously closed to certain sectors. It acknowledges the positive influence of families and teachers behind exceptional individuals. Their expectations and support were crucial in the high academic achievement of these youngsters. Despite apprehension, shame, anxiety, and other negative emotions related to inequality and social mobility, these exceptional individuals were able to integrate even in hostile elite environments. For this, they needed to overcome different costs, from catching up academically to learning other forms of less explicit cultural capital to belong to the middle class, sometimes camouflaging and sometimes becoming cultural omnivores. In this work, I emphasize a related, yet theoretically different, cost, that of building social capital.

Contrary to the expectations in such a segregated society, the SPP students made friends, and they made cross-class friends. This process was much easier in less elitist environments and when middle-class peers could act as brokers and cultural guides, lowering the relational costs of building upper-class friendships. Most of them finished their studies, despite the gaps they carried over from their elementary- and middle-school education, despite their economic, cultural, and social capital costs, and despite their overall emotional costs. Most of them are findings jobs. The majority of these individuals have indeed achieved a higher socioeconomic position, primarily attributed to their educational pursuits. However, the extent of their mobility experiences and possibilities depends a great deal on two key factors: the quality of the labor market within their chosen career and its elitism. Specifically, the weight of cultural and social capital in securing employment.

Zooming out from this study and case, methodologically, closely following individuals for a relatively long period of time that includes important transitions to adulthood and critical junctures in terms of social mobility (entering higher education, graduating, and finding employment) offers a more comprehensive and process-oriented examination of social mobility instead of only focusing on two or more life points. This study opens the black box of mobility as it is happening and as difficulties emerge, including the hidden emotions related to it. Closely following individuals ethnographically gives depth to the analysis and good quality data. This subjective and individual perspective, while occasionally emphasizing agency and strategies, strives to maintain awareness of the structural forces behind opportunities and costs within the broader processes of social mobility.

Theoretically, turning Tilly's (1998) durable inequalities mechanisms upside down, this Element contributes to the literature on inequality by highlighting two mechanisms behind social mobility: gate opening and diversified networks. Generating gate-opening opportunities and more diversified networks should be at the core of any project designed to foster social change toward equality. These mechanisms imply countering powerful and more inertial mechanisms that produce and reproduce inequality and immobility such as opportunity hoarding, and particularly pronounced in segregated environments characterized by high levels of social closure. Although the literature has proved (Coleman, 1988; Kaztman, 2001; Kaztman & Retamoso, 2007) that less segregated environments are a necessary condition for diversified networks to emerge and are correlated to social mobility (Chetty et al., 2022), we know less about the specific conditions under which those networks are indeed formed or how less segregated environments may lead to mobility. This Element contributes to these underspecified mechanisms in the literature showing that diversified networks can appear, even in extremely unequal contexts, but that they are far from natural. Quite the contrary, they require intense relational work (Zelizer, 2012) often carried one-sidedly by the underprivileged.

Regarding the mechanisms through which less segregated environments may lead toward mobility, this Element poses diversified networks (both direct ties and exposure to them) at the center. By diversified networks, however, I understand having not only upper-class linkages but also middle- and same-class linkages. Connections to peers and, especially, professors with more resources bring information and opportunities to less privileged students. While those with more resources have more information or opportunities to give away, middle-class connections also play a crucial role, because they can be brokers generating ties between those at the bottom and those at the top and they can act as cultural guides (Lareau, 2015) to the latter. Interestingly and perhaps more revealing to the theory, same-class connections in less segregated environments can be just as useful as cross-class connections for those aiming to move up the social ladder. Same-class friends in mixed environments combine access to opportunities with the ability to provide more effective support due to their closer relationships to others undergoing similar situations as themselves. Hence, diverse ties, in terms of resources and strength, appear to be the best combination for social mobility to take place, and to do so more smoothly. Finally, diverse networks might act indirectly, through exposure to information, higher expectations, and role models that may lead toward social mobility.

Despite the study being conducted at one institution in one country, its theoretical validity goes further. The institution and the country are cases of extreme inequality and segregation. These scope conditions are ideal theoretically to prove what can be done against inequality and segregation. If mobility and some degree of class integration were possible in this unequal context, it should be even more possible in less unequal and less segregated contexts. An important scope condition for diverse networks to emerge might be the merit base of the program. When Allport (1954) developed the "contact hypothesis," he suggested the benefits of increased contact for lowering inter-group prejudice, *under conditions of equality for the subjects*. Merit empowered lower-class individuals by instilling in them a sense of pride and a clear sense of deservingness. Simultaneously, it acted as a magnet for social interaction, drawing others to befriend them, work with them, or, at the very least, recognize them as good students and potential good workers. Although a meta-analysis of contact hypothesis (Pettigrew & Tropp, 2006) suggests that the equality condition is not a necessary one, we do not know whether these results would hold if lower-class students entered through different criteria, such as only an income threshold.

Conversely, explorations in less elitist contexts, such as public universities, suggest lower relational costs for social integration (Corredor et al., 2020a). Similar patterns have been observed for other contexts (Aries & Seider, 2005). The extent to which different types of institutions yield similar trajectories of mobility and, ultimately, whether enduring higher relational costs was worthwhile or not remains to be explored by comparing salaries and other well-being measures. Finally, the collective experience of this program, where many "outsiders," underprivileged students in this case, entered together, created a critical mass for them to identify with and feel protected. While, as mentioned before, there was not much collective pride in the experience as there is in other experiences, such as Afro diversity programs in the United States, the size effect could have also been crucial in facilitating some level of integration.

Despite this Element's focus on social capital and mobility, the evidence comprised in it also poses some theoretical questions, if not definite answers, to other important concepts related to mobility. On the one hand, it shows a less significant presence of the divided habitus described by the literature in other contexts. The difficult and sometimes painful experience of the studied youth trajectories are often shared with families and, at least, some friends. Many become main providers in their families of origin or at least play a crucial role in helping mothers, grandmothers, and siblings. This, coupled with the high mobility expectations and support of families of origin, seems to impact these upwardly mobile young professionals differently than in other contexts. This seems to make the divided habitus and moral conflicts (Bourdieu, 2007; Friedman, 2016; Lehmann, 2014; Morton, 2019) less pronounced. Despite the initial effort to camouflage and avoid standing out, as described earlier, most of them gradually find a way to navigate between two worlds, becoming culturally omnivorous. Unlike other contexts (Gaztambide-Fernández, 2009), they do not end up assimilating or believing they are part of the elite. They cannot. They cannot leave families behind, and they will always face otherness in such a class unequal society.

On the other hand, this Element sheds light on some nontraditional cultural capital traits that may foster social mobility. A traditional approach to social mobility through cultural capital typically involves learning and assimilating cultural capital from those at the top. This is a deficit perspective that places blame on individuals at the bottom for lacking the required cultural capital and emphasizes the need for them to acquire it. However, this Element not only demonstrates the processes of learning, assimilation, and camouflaging but also highlights how certain cultural traits that lower-class students bring from their background are crucial for their social mobility, and for reducing its costs. *Rebusque*, a strategy involving diverse economic activities to combat the fear of falling, is one such trait.

In terms of policy implications, studies of the role of education in social mobility oscillate between positive and negative outcomes. The positive ones emphasize the equalizing role of college. The negative ones emphasize the barriers to access the best institutions, the costs of surviving in them, or the new barriers that appear in the labor market. This study undoubtedly shows positive results in terms of social mobility. It insists on the power of opportunity, especially educational opportunities.

Indeed, it becomes unavoidable to contemplate the loss of talent in our societies when the majority is denied access to better opportunities. Without programs like the analyzed SPP program in Colombia, or any viable alternatives, we are losing at least about 10,000 future doctors, scientists, psychologists, and lawyers annually. The actual loss is likely greater, because this program only targeted those that needed minimal assistance – individuals who had already navigated numerous barriers in the funnel of social mobility, developed a mobility habitus, and possessed a strong belief in education as a pathway to social mobility. There is an opportunity to do much more by opening doors earlier, perhaps in middle school, elementary school, and in early childhood programs, including maternal health. How much talent are we forfeiting every year in our uneven continent? It is perhaps important to zoom even further and recognize that this is not only relevant for the poor; it is relevant for the growth of all. To expand the size of the pie that we can later redistribute, we need increased productivity, and that requires more human capital.

Simultaneously, this work also highlights the costs and limitations of social mobility even for exceptional individuals in exceptional contexts. There is significant room for improvement, and institutions should consciously work to alleviate these costs. For example, educational institutions could facilitate the formation of more cross-class ties among students, given the relevance that diversified networks have for social mobility. They can also strive to make their hidden curriculum more explicit, avoiding assumptions about students possessing middle- or upper-middle-class capital. Teaching labor market searching skills and improving connections with the labor market for first-generation students is another strategy universities can adopt to ease the transition for them. The labor market, in turn, could serve as either a great equalizer or a source of new inequalities, depending on many factors. Its demand for professionals is particularly significant, and education alone may not be sufficient. If highly qualified individuals, who invested substantial effort in their studies and raised their mobility expectations, encounter low-quality labor markets and struggle to find good jobs, frustration and disappointment emerge. Elitist labor markets often harbor hidden barriers that further complicate the landscape of social mobility. Diversity training in selection processes remains an area where the region lags, along with a need for conscious decisions from both private and public sectors to favor the hiring of first-generation students and other underprivileged groups. This would ensure that diversity training has a tangible impact rather than remain on paper. The resourcefulness demonstrated by the main characters in this Element should inspire this decision. There is substantial potential for action here, moving beyond merely ensuring equality of opportunities to placing greater emphasis on achieving equal outcomes. I hope this Element contributes to such conversations.

References

Abrahams, J., & Ingram, N. (2013). The chameleon habitus: Exploring local students' negotiations of multiple fields. *Sociological Research Online*, *18*(4), 1–14.

Adrianzén, M. A., Chevez, H. F., Morales, W. N., Quevedo, V., & Chiyón, S. V. (2019). Study-group diversity and early college academic outcomes: Experimental evidence from a higher education inclusion program in Peru. *Economics of Education Review*, *72*, 131–146.

Allport, G. W. (1954). *The Nature of Prejudice*: Addison.

Álvarez-Rivadulla, M. J. (2017, 06/07/2017). Ser Pilo Paga y la desigualdad en Colombia. *Red de la Educación. La Silla Vacía*. Retrieved from https://lasillavacia.com/silla-llena/red-de-la-educacion/historia/ser-pilo-paga-y-la-desigualdad-en-colombia-61289

Álvarez-Rivadulla, M. J. (2023). Clases medias en Bogotá y Montevideo. In G. Assusa & G. Benza (Eds.), *Producción y reproducción social de las desigualdades en la América Latina actual. Nuevas tendencias, disputas e identidades*. Buenos Aires/México: CLACSO-Siglo XXI Editores. CLACSO.

Álvarez-Rivadulla, M. J., Castro, C., Corredor, J., et al. (2017). *El Programa Ser Pilo Paga: Impactos iniciales en equidad en el acceso a la educación superior y el desempeño académico*. Retrieved from. https://repositorio.uniandes.edu.co/server/api/core/bitstreams/149fbc01-ada9-4e56-9099-cd339a4a3219/content

Álvarez-Rivadulla, M. J., Jaramillo, A. M., Fajardo, F., Cely, L., Molano, A., & Montes, F. (2022). College integration and social class. *Higher Education*, *84* (3)–669.

Angulo, R., Gaviria, A., Páez, G. N., & Azevedo, J. P. (2012). *Movilidad social en Colombia*. Retrieved from https://repositorio.uniandes.edu.co/server/api/core/bitstreams/560b81e2-6d2b-46b2-930e-318190583137/content

Aries, E. (2008). *Race and Class Matters at an Elite College*: Temple University Press.

Aries, E., & Seider, M. (2005). The interactive relationship between class identity and the college experience: The case of lower income students. *Qualitative Sociology*, *28*(4), 419–443.

Armstrong, E. A., & Hamilton, L. T. (2013). *Paying for the Party*: Harvard University Press.

Badel, A., & Peña, X. (2010) "Descomponiendo la brecha salarial de género con ajuste de sesgo de selección: el caso colombiano." *Revista de análisis económico, 25.2* (2010), 169–191.

Barrera-Osorio, F., & Bayona-Rodríguez, H. (2019). Signaling or better human capital: Evidence from Colombia. *Economics of Education Review, 70,* 20–34.

Bathmaker, A.-M., Ingram, N., Abrahams, J., et al. (2016). *Higher Education, Social Class and Social Mobility: The Degree Generation*: Springer.

Behrman, J. R., Gaviria, A., Székely, M., Birdsall, N., & Galiani, S. (2001). Intergenerational mobility in Latin America. *Economia*, *2*(1), 1–44.

Beller, E., & Hout, M. (2006). Welfare states and social mobility: How educational and social policy may affect cross-national differences in the association between occupational origins and destinations. *Research in Social Stratification and Mobility, 24*(4), 353–365.

Benza, G., & Kessler, G. (2020). *Uneven Trajectories: Latin American Societies in the Twenty-First Century*: Cambridge University Press.

Billingham, S. (2018). *Access to Success and Social Mobility through Higher Education: A Curate's Egg?*: Emerald Group.

Blee, K. M., & Currier, A. (2011). Ethics beyond the IRB: An introductory essay. *Qualitative Sociology, 34*, 401–413.

Bourdieu, P. (1984). *Distinction: A Social Critique of the Judgement of Taste*: Routledge.

Bourdieu, P. (2018). *The forms of capital.* In: The Sociology of Economic Life, Routledge, pp. 78–92.

Bourdieu, P. (1998). *The State Nobility: Elite Schools in the Field of Power*: Stanford University Press.

Bourdieu, P. (2007). *Sketch for a Self-analysis*, The University of Chicago Press.

Chan, T. W. (2018). Social mobility and the well-being of individuals. *The British Journal of Sociology, 69*(1), 183–206.

Chetty, R., Friedman, J. N., Saez, E., Turner, N., & Yagan, D. (2020). Income segregation and intergenerational mobility across colleges in the United States. The Quarterly Journal of Economics, *135*(3): 1567–1633.

Chetty, R., Jackson, M. O., Kuchler, T., et al. (2022). Social capital I: Measurement and associations with economic mobility. *Nature, 608*(7921), 108–121.

Coleman, J. S. (1988). Social capital in the creation of human capital. *American Journal of Sociology, 94*, S95–S120.

Corredor, J., and Álvarez Rivadulla, M.J. (2024). The elephant in the (class) room: Cultural capital as personal differences and college segregation [Manuscript submitted for publication]

Corredor, J., Álvarez-Rivadulla, M. J., & Maldonado-Carreño, C. (2020a). Good will hunting: Social integration of students receiving forgivable loans for college education in contexts of high inequality. *Studies in Higher Education*, *45*(8)1664–1678.

Corredor, J., González-Arango, F., & Maldonado-Carreño, C. (2020b). When unintended effects are really unintended: Depressive symptoms and other psychological effects of forgivable loan programs for college education. *Higher Education*, *80*(4):645–662.

Cotler, J. (2016). *Educación superior e inclusión social: Un estudio cualitativo de los becarios del programa Beca 18*: Ministerio de Educación.

Crozier, G., Reay, D., & Clayton, J. (2019). Working the Borderlands: Working-class students constructing hybrid identities and asserting their place in higher education. *British Journal of Sociology of Education*, *40*(7), 922–937.

Díaz Vargas, L. M. (2013). De aquí a mañana: Expectativas a futuro en jóvenes de la Comuna IV de Soacha.

Ehrenreich, B. (2020). *Fear of Falling: The Inner Life of the Middle Class*: Hachette UK.

Espinoza, Ó. , & González, L. E. (2016). La educación superior en Chile y la compleja transición desde el régimen de autofinanciamiento hacia el régimen de gratuidad. *Revista Latinoamericana de Educación Comparada: RELEC*, *7* (10), 35–51.

Ferguson, S., & Lareau, A. (2018). *First-generation College Students in Elite Setting: Patterns of Cultural Exclusion*. Department of Sociology, University of Pennsylvania. Unpublished paper.

Ferreyra, M. M., Avitabile, C., & Paz, F. H. (2017). *At a Crossroads: Higher Education in Latin America and the Caribbean*: World Bank.

Friedman, S. (2012). Cultural omnivores or culturally homeless? Exploring the shifting cultural identities of the upwardly mobile. *Poetics*, *40*(5), 467–489.

Friedman, S. (2014). The price of the ticket: Rethinking the experience of social mobility. *Sociology*, *48*(2), 352–368.

Friedman, S. (2016). Habitus clivé and the emotional imprint of social mobility. *The Sociological Review*, *64*(1), 129–147.

Friedman, S., & Laurison, D. (2019). *The Class Ceiling: Why It Pays to Be Privileged*: Policy Press.

García Villegas, Mauricio, and Laura Quiroz López. (2011). Apartheid educativo: educación, desigualdad e inmovilidad social en Bogotá. Revista de Economía Institucional 13(25): 137–162.

García-Villegas, M., & López, L. Q. (2011). Apartheid educativo. Educación, desigualdad e inmovilidad social en Bogotá. *Revista de Economía Institucional*, *13*(25).

García, S., Rodríguez, C., Sánchez, F., & Bedoya, J. G. (2015). *La lotería de la cuna: La movilidad social a través de la educación en los municipios de Colombia*. Retrieved from https://repositorio.uniandes.edu.co/server/api/core/bitstreams/1fdc7134-c57c-4d03-a4f0-9268b9c7d377/content

García-Villegas, M., Cárdenas, J. C., & Fergusson, L. (2021). *La quinta puerta*: Ariel Colombia.

Gaztambide-Fernández, R. A. (2009). *The Best of the Best: Becoming Elite at an American Boarding School*: Harvard University Press.

Granfield, R. (1991). Making it by faking it: Working-class students in an elite academic environment. *Journal of Contemporary Ethnography, 20*(3), 331–351.

Granovetter, M. S. (1977). The strength of weak ties. *American Journal of Sociology, 78*(6), 347–367.

Gray, B., & Kish-Gephart, J. J. (2013). Encountering social class differences at work: How "class work" perpetuates inequality. *Academy of Management Review, 38*(4), 670–699.

Hertz, T., Jayasundera, T., Piraino, P., Selcuk, S., Smith, N., & Verashchagina, A. (2007). The inheritance of educational inequality: International comparisons and fifty-year trends. *The BE Journal of Economic Analysis & Policy, 7* (2):1–30.

Ingram, N., Bathmaker, A.-M., Abrahams, J., et al. (2023). *The Degree Generation: The Making of Unequal Graduate Lives*: Policy Press.

Jack, A. A. (2016). (No) harm in asking: Class, acquired cultural capital, and academic engagement at an elite university. *Sociology of Education, 89*(1), 1–19.

Jack, A. A. (2019). *The Privileged Poor: How Elite Colleges Are Failing Disadvantaged Students*: Harvard University Press.

Kaztman, R. (2001). Seducidos y abandonados: El aislamiento social de los pobres urbanos. *Revista de la Cepal 75*.

Kaztman, R. (2023). [Comunicación Personal].

Kaztman, R., & Retamoso, A. (2007). Efectos de la segregación urbana sobre la educación en Montevideo. *Revista de la CEpal, 91*(133): 133–153.

Khan, S. (2011). *Privilege: The Making of an Adolescent Elite at St. Paul's School*: Princeton University Press.

Lareau, A. (2011). *Unequal Childhoods: Class, Race, and Family Life*: Univ of California Press.

Lareau, A. (2015). Cultural knowledge and social inequality. *American Sociological Review, 80*(1), 1–27.

Lee, E. M. (2016). *Class and Campus Life: Managing and Experiencing Inequality at an Elite College*: Cornell University Press.

Lee, E. M., & Harris, J. (2020). *Counterspaces, Counterstructures: Low-income, First-generation, and Working-class Students' Peer Support at Selective Colleges 1*. Paper presented at the Sociological Forum.

Lee, E. M., & Kramer, R. (2013). Out with the old, in with the new? Habitus and social mobility at selective colleges. *Sociology of Education*, *86*(1), 18–35.

Lehmann, W. (2014). Habitus transformation and hidden injuries: Successful working-class university students. *Sociology of Education*, *87*(1), 1–15.

Londoño-Vélez, J. (2011). Movilidad social, preferencias redistributivas y felicidad en Colombia. *Desarrollo y Sociedad*, *68*, 171–212.

Londoño-Vélez, J., Rodríguez, C., & Sánchez, F. (2020). Upstream and downstream impacts of college merit-based financial aid for low-income students: Ser Pilo Paga in Colombia. *American Economic Journal: Economic Policy*, *12*(2), 193–227.

Londoño-Vélez, J., Rodríguez, C., Sánchez, F., & Álvarez, L. E. (2023). *Financial Aid and Social Mobility: Evidence From Colombia's Ser Pilo Paga* (No. w31737). National Bureau of Economic Research. Retrieved from https://www.nber.org/system/files/working_papers/w31737/w31737.pdf

Manzoni, A., & Streib, J. (2019). The equalizing power of a college degree for first-generation college students: Disparities across institutions, majors, and achievement levels. *Research in Higher Education*, *60*(5), 577–605.

Medina, Pablo, Natalia Ariza, Pablo Navas, Fernando Rojas, Gina Parody, Juan Alejandro Valdivia et al. (2018). An unintended effect of financing the university education of the most brilliant and poorest Colombian students: The case of the intervention of the Ser Pilo Paga program. *Complexity*, *2018*: 1–9.

Méndez, M. L., & Gayo, M. (2018). *Upper Middle Class Social Reproduction: Wealth, Schooling, and Residential Choice in Chile*: Springer.

Morton, J. M. (2019). Moving up without losing your way. *Moving Up without Losing Your Way*: Princeton University Press.

Neal, J. W. (2010). Hanging out: Features of urban children's peer social networks. *Journal of Social and Personal Relationships*, *27*(7), 982–1000.

Pettigrew, T. F., & Tropp, L. R. (2006). A meta-analytic test of intergroup contact theory. *Journal of Personality and Social Psychology*, *90*(5), 751.

Pinzón Flechas, P.C., & Álvarez Rivadulla, M. J. (2023). "Los beneficiarios de ser pilo paga en el mercado laboral: experiencias de movilidad social, incertidumbre y recursividad." *Análisis Político*, *36*(107): 53–88.

Quacquarelli-Symonds. (2022). *QS World University Rankings*. Retrieved from https://www.topuniversities.com/qs-world-university-rankings

Reay, D. (2000). A useful extension of Bourdieu's conceptual framework?: Emotional capital as a way of understanding mothers' involvement in their children's education? *The Sociological Review*, *48*(4), 568–585.

Reay, D. (2005). Beyond consciousness? The psychic landscape of social class. *Sociology, 39*(5), 911–928.

Reay, D., Crozier, G., & Clayton, J. (2009). "Strangers in paradise"? Working-class students in elite universities. *Sociology, 43*(6), 1103–1121.

Rivera, L. A. (2016). *Pedigree: How Elite Students Get Elite Jobs*: Princeton University Press.

Robbins, S. B., Lauver, K., Le, H., Davis, D., Langley, R., & Carlstrom, A. (2004). Do psychosocial and study skill factors predict college outcomes? A meta-analysis. *Psychological Bulletin, 130*(2), 261.

Rodríguez Anaiz, P. C. (2023). *Segregated Inclusion: An Intersectional Analysis of Working-class Women's Experiences at an Elite University*: UCL (University College London).

Rodríguez, P., & Archer, L. (2022). Reproducing privilege through whiteness and beauty: An intersectional analysis of elite Chilean university students' practices. *British Journal of Sociology of Education, 43*(5), 804–822.

Royster, D. (2003). *Race and the Invisible Hand: How White Networks Exclude Black Men from Blue-collar Jobs*: Univ. of California Press.

Rubin, M., Evans, O., & Wilkinson, R. B. (2016). A longitudinal study of the relations among university students' subjective social status, social contact with university friends, and mental health and well-being. *Journal of Social and Clinical Psychology, 35*(9), 722–737.

Saraví, G. (2015). *Juventudes Fragmentadas*: CIESAS.

Scott, J., & Marshall, G. (2009). *Cultural Capital*: Oxford University Press.

Sennett, R., & Cobb, J. (1972). *The Hidden Injuries of Class*: Vintage.

Sherman, R. (2017). *Uneasy Street: The Anxieties of Affluence*: Princeton University Press.

SNIES. (2021). *Sistema Nacional de Información de la Educación Superior*: Ministerio de Educación Nacional.

Streib, J. (2017). The unbalanced theoretical toolkit: Problems and partial solutions to studying culture and reproduction but not culture and mobility. *American Journal of Cultural Sociology, 5*(1), 127–153.

Stuber, J. M. (2011). *Inside the College Gates: How Class and Culture Matter in Higher Education*: Lexington Books.

Telles, E. (2014). *Pigmentocracies: Ethnicity, Race, and Color in Latin America*: UNC Press Books.

Tilly, C. (1998). *Durable Inequality*: University of California.

Torche, F. (2011). Is a college degree still the great equalizer? Intergenerational mobility across levels of schooling in the United States. *American Journal of Sociology, 117*(3), 763–807.

Torche, F. (2014). Intergenerational mobility and inequality: The Latin American case. *Annual Review of Sociology*, *40*, 619–642.

Uribe Mallarino, C., & Pardo Perez, C. (2006). La ciudad vivida: Movilidad espacial y representaciones sobre la estratificación social en Bogotá. *Universitas Humanistica*, *62*, 169–203. Retrieved from http://www.javeriana.edu.co/Facultades/C_Sociales/universitas/62/uribe.pdf

Urrea, F., Viáfara, C., & Viveros, M. (2014). From whitened miscegenation to tri-ethnic multiculturalism. Race and ethnicity in Colombia. *Pigmentocracies. Ethnicity, Race, and Color in Latin America*: The University of North Carolina Press, 81–125.

Valente, R. R., & Berry, B. J. (2017). Performance of students admitted through affirmative action in Brazil. *Latin American Research Review*, *52*(1), 18–34.

Viáfara López, C. A. (2017). Movilidad social intergeneracional de acuerdo al color de la piel en Colombia. *Sociedad y Economía*, *33*, 263–287.

Vigoya, M. V., & Hernández, F. G. (2010). Género y generación en las experiencias de ascenso social de personas negras en Bogotá. *Maguaré*, *24*, 99–130.

Viveros Vigoya, M. (2022). *El oxímoron de las clases medias negras: Movilidad social e interseccionalidad en Colombia*: Bielefeld University Press.

World Bank (2021). World Bank, Poverty and Inequality Platform. The World Bank Data. https://data.worldbank.org/indicator/SI.POV.GINI

Zelizer, V. (2012). How I became a relational economic sociologist and what does that mean? *Politics & Society*, *40*(2), 145–174.

Zelizer, V., & Gaydosh, L. (2019, 01/09/2019). Class on campus. *Princeton Alumni Weekly*. Retrieved from https://paw.princeton.edu/article/essay-class-campus

Acknowledgements

This Element has an unsolvable writing style challenge. It is written in the first person, intentionally altering between singular and plural. It is not a mistake. Rather, it reflects the collaborative nature of this eight-year research endeavor. I want to acknowledge the work of several committed research assistants, whom I met when they were undergraduate or MA students, most of whom became engaged coauthors: Paola Camelo, Diana Viáfara, Mariana Vargas, Felipe Fajardo, Ana María Jaramillo, Laura Cely, Paula Pinzón, Maria Paula Gutiérrez, Andrés Galeano and Juan Sebastián Gómez. Weekly meetings with them throughout these years, sitting on my office floor, discussing each interview together, coding, ethical issues, and relevant bibliography were the highlight of my weeks and of my career. Seeing them grow as researchers, teaching me things, passionately drawing two-by-two tables on my whiteboard were invaluable learning experiences for all of us.

My discussions with Javier Corredor, wise colleague, friend, and co-author, played a pivotal role in shaping this project. Presenting initial ideas for this Element in Santiago and Montevideo provided enlightening perspectives on the peculiarities of the case and the patterns that emerge in the region. I thank Emmanuelle Barozet, Maria Luisa Méndez, and all the participants in the Instituto de Estudios Urbanos' Seminar in Santiago as well as the organizers and attendees of the Miradas Históricas y Contemporáneas sobre la Desigualdad y la Pobreza en Uruguay y América Latina seminar at Universidad de la República in Montevideo.

My two lifelong mentors, Ruben Kaztman and John Markoff, meticulously reviewed and provided feedback on early drafts of this Element and, as always, identified what I wanted to convey before I did myself. Javier Auyero's incisive comments and questions helped me push my argument further. Viviana Zelizer encouraged me to keep writing because she believed I was doing something different from current trends in US Sociology. Her words and kind comments motivated me tremendously to continue writing despite other responsibilities. My Sociology community at Universidad de los Andes provided the intellectual environment to work on this project, and the emotional support to keep writing while simultaneously teaching and chairing the department. Universidad de los Andes itself not only provided funds to hire research assistants throughout fieldwork but has also shown great receptivity to the research results, even when they where unconfortable for signaling things to improve in our institutional ways of dealing with diversity and inequality, or in our hidden curriculum enmeshed in a classist society.

I am grateful to my series editor at Cambridge Elements, Victoria Murillo, and two anonymous reviewers who offered valuable, targeted, and insightful feedback. Juan Carlos, Martin, and my family in Uruguay, as always, have been my pillars of support in life and my cheerleaders when I need them. Thanks.

Cambridge Elements

Politics and Society in Latin America

Advisory Board

About the series

Latin American politics and society are at a crossroads, simultaneously confronting serious challenges and remarkable opportunities that are likely to be shaped by formal institutions and informal practices alike. The Elements series on Politics and Society in Latin America offers multidisciplinary and methodologically pluralist contributions on the most important topics and problems confronted by the region

Cambridge Elements

Politics and Society in Latin America

Elements in the series

A full series listing is available at: www.cambridge.org/PSLT

For EU product safety concerns, contact us at Calle de José Abascal, 56–1°, 28003 Madrid, Spain or eugpsr@cambridge.org.

www.ingramcontent.com/pod-product-compliance
Ingram Content Group UK Ltd.
Pitfield, Milton Keynes, MK11 3LW, UK
UKHW022145080726
473066UK00010B/768

* 9 7 8 1 0 0 9 5 0 3 2 3 5 *